I0049720

$martEssentials®

for

REAL ESTATE
INVESTING

More Titles In Best-Selling SMART ESSENTIALS® Series

SMART ESSENTIALS® FOR SELLING YOUR HOME
How To Get The Highest Price In The Shortest Time

SMART ESSENTIALS® FOR BUYING A HOME
How To Get The Best Price And The Lowest Payment

SMART ESSENTIALS® FOR REAL ESTATE INVESTING
How To Build Wealth In Rental Property Today

SMART ESSENTIALS® FOR BUYING FORECLOSURES
Finding Hidden Bargains For Home Or Profit

SMART ESSENTIALS® FOR COLLEGE RENTALS
Parent And Investor Guide To Buying College-Town Real Estate

$martEssentials®

for

REAL ESTATE INVESTING

How To Build Wealth In Rental Property Today

Dan Gooder Richard

Inkspiration Media

SMART ESSENTIALS® FOR REAL ESTATE INVESTING
How To Build Wealth In Rental Property Today

Published by
Inkspiration Media
2724 Dorr Avenue, Suite 103, Fairfax, VA 22031
http://www.SmartEssentials.com

Copyright © 2014 by Inkspiration Media. All rights reserved.
ISTC: A0320120000B475D
Library of Congress Control Number: 2012923087

Publisher's Cataloging-In-Publication Data
(Prepared by The Donohue Group, Inc.)

Richard, Dan Gooder, 1947–
    Smart Essentials for real estate investing : how to build wealth in rental property today / Dan Gooder Richard.
        p. ; cm. — (Smart Essentials series)
    ISBN-13: 978-1-939319-03-6 (pbk.)
    ISBN-10: 1-939319-03-X (pbk.)
    ISBN-13: 978-1-939319-08-1 (hardcover)
    ISBN-10: 1-939319-08-0 (hardcover)
    1. Real estate investment — United States. 2. Rental housing —
United States. 3. Residential real estate — Purchasing—United States.
I. Title. II. Title: Real estate investing
HD259 .R532 2014
643/.12/0973   2012923087

No part of this publication may be reproduced, stored in a retrieval system, or transmitted in any form or by any means, electronic, mechanical, photocopying, recording, scanning, or otherwise without prior written permission of the publisher. For information on bulk purchases or corporate premium sales, please contact the Special Sales Department. Email *Investing@SmartEssentials.com*, call (703) 698-7750 or write Inkspiration Media, LLC, 2724 Dorr Avenue, Suite 103, Fairfax, VA 22031.

Trademarks: INKSPIRATION MEDIA, SMART ESSENTIALS, SMART ESSENTIALS logo, the slogan GET SMARTER FOR LESS, are trademarks of Inkspiration Media, LLC and/or its affiliates in the United States and other countries, and may not be used without written permission. All other trademarks are the property of their respective owners.

The author, editor and publisher have made every effort to ensure information in this book is accurate and complete at press time. The information, however, may not apply to your particular situation or in your state or local jurisdiction. We are not engaged in rendering legal, accounting or other professional services. Readers are urged to consult a professional for expert advice. Neither the publisher nor the author shall be liable for loss of profit or other damages, including but not limited to special, incidental, consequential, or other damages.

CONTENTS

UPFRONT

Millions of homeowners lost their houses to foreclosure in recent years—actual repossessions not just default filings or auction notices—and more will follow from the millions of underwater families who are behind on their mortgages.

Also, fueling the boom in rental demand is waves of aging baby boomers (10,000 a day are turning 65) who are downsizing and many opting to rent. More than 3 million boomerangers...young adults who lived with their parents during the Great Recession...are now moving out to rent on their own. Plus, new immigrants by the hundreds of thousands every year are renting until they can buy into the American dream of homeownership.

Simply put, millions of new renters will fill rental housing for years to come.

Why is this important?

Today's convergence of unprecedented rental demand and affordable inventory, low interest rates and higher rents has created a once-in-a-generation "Perfect Storm" of opportunity for investors in the single-family rental market. Get rich quick schemes are still too good to be true—and are mostly bunk. Today *get rich slowly* strategies are paying off handsomely for smart real estate investors.

SMART ESSENTIALS FOR REAL ESTATE INVESTING is written for the small investor. If you plan to invest in single-family homes, condos/co-ops, townhomes, duplexes, triplexes, quads or small apartment buildings with 2–10 units, this SMART ESSENTIALS is for you.

Get Smarter For Less

We know you're smart. (Reading **SMART ESSENTIALS FOR REAL ESTATE INVESTING** proves it . . . at least to us.) We know our readers are busy, capable people stressed by the fact that you only get one chance to get it right buying or selling an investment property. You appreciate smart, practical, distilled information. Your time is precious.

1

What You'll Take Away

Read this no-fluff SMART ESSENTIALS guide first. If you still want to eat the entire elephant and virtually become a professional...then this SMART ESSENTIALS guide will be your rock-solid foundation on which to build your house of knowledge. You already will have mastered smart ideas that save you thousands at the settlement table when you buy and can make you tens of thousands when you sell — plus avoid costly mistakes you didn't have to make in between.

Simply put, SMART ESSENTIALS cuts to the chase to respect your intelligence and your time.

Less Is More

We've checked the filler at the door. Side trips are not here like investing in tax liens, financing wraparound loans, noodling whether to be an accidental landlord to avoid foreclosure, flipping short sale contracts to assigned investors, sample contracts and settlement documents explained line by line, blah, blah, blah. Neither is there a glossary, index, appendix, checklists or forms. Why? Because that's what the professionals on your team are paid to know.

How This SMART ESSENTIALS Is Organized

OK. After the Blueprint gives you the Big Picture of real estate investing, there are six masteries you must get right from the start. These shape the chapters in your SMART ESSENTIALS guide:

- **TOOLKIT:** Know the rules to maximize cash flow, tax breaks and investment return.

- **PROPERTIES:** Find properties that make money both when you buy and when you sell.

- **ANALYZE:** Run the numbers to spot diamonds in the rough that handsomely provide cash flow.

- **PURCHASE:** Craft win-win counteroffers and nail down financing that fits your strategy.

- **MANAGE:** Avoid costly property management mistakes poor landlords make.

- **CASH OUT:** Know the triggers to time your exit and get out for the most profit possible.

Niche Strategies And This SMART ESSENTIALS Guide

Much can be written (and has been) about specialized investing strategies designed to chase esoteric investment niches:

● Some investors specialize in short sales, auctions, tax sales, HUD foreclosures (U.S. Department of Housing and Urban Development), bank-owned foreclosures ("real estate owned" REOs), probate sales, flipping properties or contracts to buy.

● Other strategies target specific tenant markets: rent-to-own, student housing, subsidized housing (Section 8 Voucher) or subsidized renters such as seniors or disabled.

● Even more strategic niches exist for developer/builders: rehab to sell, converting assets (apartments to condos), adding extra units or buy-small-and-expand, finding new uses to repurpose residential into commercial property, subdividing land, profiting from financing the properties sold.

● Then there are the Rich Guys. Big money investors gobble up large multi-family apartment buildings (11–49 units) or apartment communities (50+ unit facilities) or commercial property for office, retail, industrial, warehouse, hotel, restaurant, gas or convenience, or become a developer.

That is, of course, oversimplifying investment strategy niches.

Yes, these specialties all offer their own opportunities — and risks — and deserve in-depth books in themselves. That is why you will only find these specialty niches mentioned in passing in this concise SMART ESSENTIALS FOR REAL ESTATE INVESTING.

This SMART ESSENTIALS is for the small residential investor who wants to know how to build personal wealth with single-family rental property in today's market.

Most Important We Want To Hear From You. Often.

Nothing informs our readers as much as stories from other Smarties . . . what they did right, mistakes they can laugh at (now) and advice on tricky choices they had to make along the road of good intentions. Come back regularly to our website at *http://www.SmartEssentials.com*. Share your experience. Lurk over the amazing tips and challenges other Smarties experienced. Tell us how we can do better in the next edition. (We're smart but we're not perfect. Yet.) We love your stories! And, we know other Smarties do too.

Smart Essentials

Page   **Essential Note**

BLUEPRINT

Let's cut to the chase. There are only two types of real estate investors: "Flippers" looking for a fast buck and "landlords" looking to hold for the long term. For starters: Good rentals — underpriced properties that rent easily and need only paint and carpet — are a rare find. Experienced investors scoop them up before rookies even know they're on the market. To win as a patient-money investor, you must be quick (think whack-a-mole), informed and ready for market ups and downs.

On the other hand, if you get it wrong you can end up in the disaster of bankruptcy. Murphy says what can go wrong will go wrong in real estate for the unprepared:

▶ Unforeseen bust in value of your property;

▶ Blindsided by unexpected big expenses;

▶ A sudden shift in neighborhood character; or

▶ An unexpected need for cash that forces an early sale.

Being keenly aware of these risks is the best way to avoid them. Opportunities for savvy investors are everywhere in today's market — if you know where to look. Good properties don't linger. That's why the biggest rewards today favor decisive action.

3 KEYS TO REAL ESTATE INVESTING IN TODAY'S MARKET

Can real estate pay off in an era of low inflation and relatively low appreciation?

Yes. If you are smart.

It bears repeating: Real estate investing is an opportunity now caused by the mix of a unique cocktail of:

▶ Low prices (driven down by recession and foreclosures).

▶ Low interest rates (kept low for the same reasons plus government policy).

▶ High demand for rentals from millions of new families and former owners who lost their homes to foreclosure.

That jet-fuel investment mix makes buying single-family rentals today an exceptional opportunity for the smart investor. You can buy one or two houses or apartments and still generate returns that will make you smile all the way to the bank.

How?

Successful real estate investors enjoy supplemental monthly income, earn additional tax benefits and use other people's money (OPM) to underwrite the venture. Then, renters contribute to investors' mortgage payments while investors' equity grows — yielding capital gains at sale time.

Today, real estate investors are increasingly moving back into the residential market. Why? Three major factors make it easier for them to cover their costs — even generate income immediately — from owning rental properties.

1. Value

Investors are seeing great values in the lowest home prices in a generation — and they know how to buy them. During the boom years of the housing market, many investors bought and sold for a quick profit — which can still happen with some properties in some areas. Today, smart investors are renting out property for passive rental income. Month after month, cash comes into their bank accounts, building their wealth with someone else's money.

2. Demand

Not only are there great values to be found in foreclosed homes, many areas are experiencing increased demand for rentals and higher rental prices — particularly at the lower end of the market — due to people having lost their homes to foreclosure.

According to the report by the Joint Center for Housing Studies at Harvard University, "America's Rental Housing: The Key to a Balanced National Policy," more households are competing for low-cost rental units due to homeowners losing their homes to foreclosure and renters being evicted from houses their landlords lost to foreclosure. In addition, the housing recession saw fewer new home and multi-family units built than in the boom years.

Quite simply, as the U.S. population continues to grow, the strong demand for housing will continue into the foreseeable future, which tees up an investment opportunity for you. In essence, America is facing a housing shortage.

3. Interest rates	Today's very affordable interest rates help minimize the cost of investing in residential real estate. But today's rates won't last forever — making now a great time to buy an investment property.

TOP 10 PROVEN SECRETS TO SUCCESS

Of course, success is not a sure thing for any investor/landlord. To turn a rental property into a moneymaker requires:

▶ Timely and accurate information
▶ Careful planning
▶ Smart property selection
▶ Enlightened management
▶ Cashing out at the right time

There are nearly as many investment-hunting strategies as there are investors. Yet experience provides some universal truths that pay off. Here are the top 10.

1. Compare Comparables (Know Your Market)	Use sales prices of nearby comparable properties to get the truest sense of market value. Do the same for area rents. A low price can be supported by a reasonable rent; but, remember, renters who can afford a high rent can afford to buy instead.

2. Tax Laws Change	A good investment is a good investment before it's a good tax shelter. Tax laws change. The right property in the right place with the right financing and right management will weather inevitable tax-code changes.

3. Specialize	Start in a market segment you're comfortable with. Whether you focus on fixer-uppers, foreclosures, starter homes, low-down-payment properties,

condominiums, student housing, or small apartment buildings, over time you'll benefit from experience by specializing in one aspect of investment real estate properties.

4. Run The Numbers

Operating expenses from repairs and maintenance, loan payments, taxes, vacancy costs and more will determine the difference between smooth sailing and a sinking ship. Up-front number crunching is your best strategy. Run before-tax and after-tax cash-flow statements with confirmed figures, not wide-eyed guesses. (We'll show you how in Chapter 4: ANALYZE.) It's more than just income in and monthly payment out.

5. Determine Last Rent Increase

If you're buying an investment property with tenants already in place, check if the rents were recently increased, which could limit your future income. Worse still, tenants might decide to move. Check the date of the last increase to know where you stand. Also, make sure current tenant doesn't have a short-term lease, living there simply to tempt the unsuspecting investor buyer. Examine existing leases and be sure to get tenants' security deposits from the seller at closing.

6. Check Tax Assessment

A current assessment that will increase after your purchase — because it is old or doesn't include unrecorded improvements — could change your property tax expenses.

7. Investigate Insurance

If seller's coverage is based on lower-than-current replacement value, your insurance cost may increase when you pay a higher purchase price.

8. Confirm Utility Costs

Ask the local utilities to verify recent utility expenses, especially if any of those costs are included in your tenant's rent.

9. Ask Your Accountant

Especially on the tax questions, as well as your basic investment analysis, be sure to get a second opinion from your tax advisor or CPA.

10. Inspect, Inspect, Inspect

Never buy a property sight unseen. Nothing replaces on-site inspection and nosing around the property like a bloodhound. Hire professional inspectors for structural and mechanical system opinions.

5 ESSENTIALS TO BUILDING WEALTH WITH REAL ESTATE INVESTING

With a relatively modest amount of capital and income, you can profit from real estate investing—once you recognize the chief elements of the rental-property marketplace (more details in a moment).

If you've bought your own home, you already know many of the financial advantages of real estate ownership. Here's a brief overview of the 5 essential ways you can profit from owning rental real estate today.

1. Lower Your Taxes

Taxes may be inevitable, but they are also controllable. In rental properties, you currently benefit from cash deductions for financing, management and operating costs as well as non-cash deductions for depreciation. You also benefit from possible lower long-term capital-gains tax rates or tax deferral.

2. Pocket Positive Cash Flow

"Positive cash flow" means income either before or after taxes. A shrewd investor knows how to turn "negative cash flow" into positive by maximizing rent through various strategies and depreciation deductions.

3. Use Leverage

Leverage involves multiplying your profits by financing as much of your investment as possible and reducing your down payment, thereby limiting the amount of cash tied up and increasing your tax deductions.

4. Benefit From Appreciation

Appreciation—an increase in property value over your purchase price—depends on finding property in a location where prices are on the rise or are likely to rise before you sell. We're not talking sky-high appreciation rates—like in the late 1970s, mid-1980s or early 2000s—which virtually guaranteed a solid return for many real estate investors, regardless of what they purchased. What we're talking about today is a residential market in which a well-chosen, well-managed rental property of one to ten units can be the "shining star" in an investor's portfolio.

**5. Cash Out
Equity Buildup**

Equity, the difference between the property value and the remaining loan balance, brings a profit either through refinancing or sale.

Every payment from your renters pays down the principal owed on your mortgage. Over time, this loan payoff may build your equity as much — or more — than appreciation. Timing is a key consideration in cashing out for maximum equity profits, since the longer you own property, the less valuable are the tax breaks available to you.

◆ ◆ ◆

**Essential
Takeaway**

Essential Takeaway: There's no one magic formula to real estate investing. Do it your way. We're believers in buying and holding for income. We also think owning multiple properties is better than owning just one. A little more than 40% of investors purchase more than one property, according to the National Association of REALTORS ®. Cash reserves can be better spread over multiple properties, and a vacancy or two has less financial impact on multiple-property owners. You are better off buying two investment properties than a single property at a too-high price. Rarely does a property with inflated value command an inflated rent, but it does generate inflated expenses, as you'll learn in Chapter 4.

◆ ◆ ◆

ASSEMBLE YOUR TEAM OF SMART ADVISORS

No matter whether you are interested in single-family homes or small residential properties of one to ten units, you'll need a network of pros.

Why? Buying an investment property involves complexities beyond those you encounter purchasing your own home. Buying a distressed or bank-owned foreclosure presents even more issues and opportunities for mistakes — which can cost you serious money.

But, first a word: We've assumed you will need advice, either because you don't have the expertise to do it all or maybe you live out of the area, out of state or even out of the country. Thus, you need an advisory team. Naturally, if you can do any of these functions yourself, we'll assume you have a genius for a client — and you can save the professional fees too.

Here are the rules of engagement for smart professionals and what they can do for you to get the job done.

1. **Investor's real estate agent.** Successful investing starts with a top real estate professional who specializes in working with rental property investors. These pros see more deals in a month than individual investors see in a lifetime. Top investor's agents understand that every investor has a different investment strategy. They can help with all the critical elements to give you a turnkey solution by managing the following vital tasks:

- ▶ Assembling market data
- ▶ Researching rental rates
- ▶ Keeping tabs on the foreclosure market
- ▶ Conducting property searches (even for those that may not be on the open market)
- ▶ Negotiating and representing your interests
- ▶ Searching for financing and lender introductions
- ▶ Managing property
- ▶ Organizing property repairs/cleaning
- ▶ Conducting tenant searches
- ▶ Recommending an appropriate sale price when it comes time to sell.

When who represents you matters most, experience counts. Look for a top-notch agent who has worked with investors, knows how to craft a "win-win" purchase offer that a seller will accept, holds advanced certifications, such as Certified Commercial Investment Manager (CCIM), Certified Realty Investment Associate (CRIA) and may also be a certified buyer's agent as an Accredited Buyer Representative (ABR), or Certified Buyer Representative (CBR). You want someone who has experience with exactly how the local process works and who can advise you each step of the way.

The best investor-specialist agents also bring their own network of professional contacts to the table:

- ▶ Property managers
- ▶ Tax advisors and appraisers

► Attorneys
► Building inspectors and craftsmen
► Structural engineers
► Environmental specialists
► Contractors, electricians, plumbers

A super-star agent's connections are essential if your advisors don't specialize in real estate or you don't have a working relationship already with the needed professionals. *Smart Tip:* Most professional services for investment properties are tax deductible.

◆ ◆ ◆

Essential Takeaway

Essential Takeaway: *The experience of a top real estate agent costs buyers nothing. Remember, real estate agents don't get paid until a deal closes. That alone is a motivation that works in the investor's interest. Also, top agents value a lifetime association far more than a single transaction. In a nutshell, top agents want you to call them to list a property for sale later on, not just help you buy it at the outset. These agents get most of their business from satisfied referrals. That's why the top professional real estate agents go that extra distance to earn your continued confidence. That said: Blindly following advice has the potential to get you in quite a bit of trouble.*

◆ ◆ ◆

2. Accountant or tax advisor. Ignorance of tax laws is understandable — but not excusable. An experienced accountant/tax advisor will play an essential role on your team. Advice will cover everything from selecting the best depreciation method (the great equalizer), evaluating the impact of various deductions on your taxable income, advising on the best time to sell or refinance, to simply keeping the books, generating profit-and-loss reports, preparing your tax return and tracking how buying investment property affects your overall financial situation. From the beginning, you may set up a Limited Liability Corporation (LLC). Holding your investment property in a single-person LLC protects your personal assets from being tapped should someone be injured on your property.

As you know, tax laws are complex and change continually. Beyond the hypothetical case examples you'll find in this guide, many other aspects of tax rules can impact your particular situation. Your accountant/tax advisor will know about alternative minimum taxes, estate taxes, reallocation of income, imputed interest, limitations on deductions, penalties, and more.

3. **Lender.** Smart investors know from their investment analysis of a property that financing is typically the largest operating expense in most investments. That's why scouting for rentals begins with having a great lender on your side. Financing makes an enormous difference in the value of and return on your investment. If the funding door closes at commercial lenders — because their guidelines for credit score or down payment or other requirements are deal-killers — then seek out a small local bank or neighborhood credit union that gets to know you and finances your purchases. Often, the best place to go for money is where they know you best.

4. **Property manager.** Your most extensive relationship will be with your property manager. Not only will your property manager save you time and help you avoid headaches, but good property management will enhance the potential income and resale value of your property. We'll go into greater detail on the services a property manager provides in Chapter 6: MANAGE.

   Besides being the point person who acts as your eyes and ears on the property, one of the greatest values a quality property manager brings to you is his or her network of local contacts. Leasing and managing property requires dealing with a lengthy list of people from online and classified operators, prospective renters, utility companies, plumbers, carpenters, electricians, painters, pest-control services, lawn services, housekeeping companies, even accountants, lenders and attorneys.

5. **Attorney.** You'll want to consult an attorney for a spectrum of services. These can include reviewing documents and contracts, checking local zoning or other laws such as rent control and tenant/landlord rights, preparing settlement documents, approving leases and guiding you (if need be) through the eviction process or a tenant lawsuit. The right property or landlord-tenant lawyer will be a resource of information and a sounding board for many essential decisions.

6. Inspectors. The best income properties get scooped up fast, especially foreclosures, which means you must be prepared to move quickly when you see a good investment home. The trick is to avoid unseen defects that cost thousands to rehab (imagine the angry foreclosed owner who flushed cement down the toilets).If you prefer to have a home inspected before making a purchase offer — which many investors do — having inspectors lined up ahead of time will help you get the edge over competing buyers.

At the very least, you'll want to hire a general home inspector to check the structure — including evidence of fire or water damage, erosion, dry rot, etc. — and all systems — roof, electrical, plumbing, furnace/boiler, air conditioning, appliances, doors/windows and so on. Your generalist may also be certified to check for mold, radon and wood-destroying pests. You should also have contact numbers for specialists to inspect, as needed, for asbestos or lead paint, polybutylene pipes (if the property was built before 1978), formaldehyde, carbon monoxide, indoor air quality, septic system, well or water quality, and any local peculiarity such as clay soil shifting, earthquake risk, landslide/mudslide/rockslide area, toxic waste or record of past violations. You could also consider having an energy audit conducted.

7. General contractor. Though you may want to get multiple contractors' estimates later, you should have at least one general contractor at the ready to give you cost estimates for any repairs or improvements — perhaps identified by your inspectors — that would have to be made to a property before you can rent it. Essentially your contractor can set a budget that separates the fixer-uppers from money pits.

8. Insurance agent. Before getting too far down the road to an investment property, have a long talk with a trusted insurance agent in the area where you want to invest to find out what types of properties could present insurance problems. For example, you may have trouble insuring an older property that still has knob-and-tube wiring — unless you completely replace or disconnect it. Properties regularly subject to high winds, storms, flooding or earthquakes may require an expensive insurance premium — which could eat into your profits. A good insurance agent can advise you upfront about what to expect.

9. Mentor. Find a mentor who has been around the track before you. We're not talking about one of those hold-your-hand millionaire coaching schemes skimmed off a Google search for a fat check. Rather, seek out an experienced local investor — someone you can show your cash flow analysis to for insights; someone to answer questions one-on-one; someone who has walked the walk and doesn't just talk the talk. Local investment clubs, landlord associations and your real estate agent are good resources for finding a mentor.

BEFORE YOU PULL THE TRIGGER, CONSIDER ALL THE RISKS

Whether your strategy is to fix up to sell, hold and sell-or-refinance later, or hold indefinitely for income, a smart investor must weigh the risks. Though most properties tend to increase in value over time, appreciation is not guaranteed (more on ideal properties in Chapter 3: PROPERTIES). In addition, some income may be lost if renters default on payments or damage the property (more on how to avoid these property-management mistakes in Chapter 6: MANAGE).

Don't Go It Alone

Before you undertake a real estate investment, talk with professionals who have dealt with rental properties and consult a tax advisor to find out how a real estate investment would affect your particular financial situation.

◆ ◆ ◆

Essential Takeaway

*Essential Takeaway: While other investments like stocks and bonds require picking the right time to buy or sell and knowing **what** to invest in, smart rental real estate investing requires choosing **where** to buy and **how** to structure the financing. The essential secret is looking for just the right combination of low risk, high return and favorable tax treatment. There are no foolproof "rules of thumb" because your income, savings, tax bracket, goals and temperament are unique to you.*

◆ ◆ ◆

The best investment properties are never on the market for long. No investor wants to miss out on a golden opportunity. More on the fun part about how to beat the new rules of the investing game in Chapter 2: TOOLKIT.

Chapter 1 Roundup

Smart Essentials BLUEPRINT ::
What You Have Learned

▶▶ What you won't find in this SMART ESSENTIALS guide.

▶▶ 3 keys to real estate investing in today's market.

▶▶ Top 10 proven secrets to success.

▶▶ 5 essentials to wealth with real estate investing.

▶▶ Assembling your team of advisors.

▶▶ Before you pull the trigger, consider all the risks.

CHAPTER 2
TOOLKIT

In this chapter, you'll learn smart ways to:

1. Use all five essential tools to profit with rental property.

2. Avoid costly depreciation and other tax mistakes.

3. Take advantage of equity buildup to cash out when time is right.

NEW RULES OF THE GAME

Hold your horses. Before you grab your agent and gallop off to lasso some foreclosures, you need to know the new rules of the investment property game. There are a lot of rookie real estate investors out there. Many think the game is a no-brainer — simply buy property, collect rent and get rich. In today's market, that kind of simplistic thinking can be a road to ruin.

Smarter investors know success takes a more sophisticated strategy. After all, you're now the manager of a business that buys and sells real estate. Your path to wealth depends on your strategy:

🗨 **Fix-Up To Sell** requires below-market property where the value after rehab is higher than the cost of improvements. (Only about 5% of investment properties are sold within one year, according to NAR surveys.)

🗨 **Hold And Sell Or Refinance** depends on (1) beating inflation, (2) minimizing your taxes and (3) sheltering income from elsewhere while the housing market drives up prices.

🗨 **Hold For Income** requires buying good property at the lowest price possible and minimizing loan costs by adjusting your down payment to produce positive cash flow from Day One. (Half of investment buyers buy for income, the NAR reports.)

> **5 Essential Tools Every Investor Needs**

Today's nimble real estate investors use five essential tools to build wealth through rental properties. Although we touched on these tools in Chapter 1, here is the nitty gritty on (1) leverage, (2) cash flow, (3) tax advantages, (4) appreciation and (5) equity buildup. Nothing replaces hands-on doing as the best way to learn.

1. Leverage[††]

The essential rule of the leverage game is to use "Other People's Money" (OPM) as much as possible, and as little of your own as possible. That means borrowing. By reducing your down payment and financing as much as possible, leverage lets you control a large investment property with a relatively small amount of capital and income. Not only do you reduce your down payment and closing costs, you also increase your tax deductions through higher mortgage interest payments.

> [††] *Leverage*
> Leverage is defined as using borrowed money ("non-equity capital") to increase returns on equity. High leverage means a small down payment (investment), and low leverage means a large down payment. Put another way, the highest leverage possible is nothing down. The lowest leverage possible is an all-cash purchase.

Your return on invested cash is multiplied by leverage, which greatly increases your buying power through borrowing. Real estate uses leverage — other people's money — more than almost any other investment type.

How leverage works. Say you buy a single-family property for $100,000 with all cash and no loan, and then sell it for $120,000 several years later. Your $20,000 gain ($120,000 – $100,000 = $20,000) represents a 20% return on your original $100,000 cash investment ($20,000 divided by $100,000 = 20%). Not bad.

Assume, instead, you had leveraged your investment by putting only $10,000 down (10%) and financed the remaining $90,000. Naturally you gain the same $20,000 when you sell several years later for $120,000, but on a $10,000 cash investment you reap a return of 200% ($20,000 divided by $10,000 = 200%) on the same property. Even smarter! (Several factors in reality will lower your profit, such as closing costs and interest payments, but to illustrate the principle, we are keeping the numbers simple.)

How does real estate stack up against investing in stocks and bonds? Often very well, if you consider how home appreciation leverages your initial investment cost.

One clear difference is how much money investors have at stake in the ebb and flow of the investment. For stocks and bonds, a 3% increase on a $10,000 initial investment means you earn $300. In real estate, investing $10,000 as a down payment on a property grows based on the much higher value of the asset you've purchased. If your $10,000 down payment is used to purchase a $100,000 property and that home appreciates 3% in one year, for example, the value of your real estate investment increases by $3,000. Leverage, in our scenario, turns your 3% investment return into a 30% increase on your investment stake.

The key distinction between real estate and stocks is that your real estate investment changes according to the greater value of your property — the asset — rather than the lesser value of your original stake. It's all about leverage!

How much leverage is just right? The straight answer is it depends on your investment strategy. A small down payment means higher monthly payments on a larger loan. For high-tax-bracket investors, the higher interest deductions can be an advantage. Conversely, a large down payment means lower monthly payments meaning higher income beyond expenses ("positive cash flow"). If generating income is your strategy, higher cash up-front and lower leverage pays off.

Avoid The Costly Mistake Of Negative Leverage

Mistake: While leveraged investments can multiply your profits, be aware if the market turns south, leverage can multiply losses. In recent markets where property values dropped, negative leverage drove some investors out of the market. Here's a stunning example: You purchase a property for $100,000 with a 10% down payment. Property values drop and you are forced to sell the property — on which you still owe $90,000 — for $80,000 — its current market value. The sale wipes out your $10,000 investment (down payment), plus you have to put $10,000 more on the table to pay off the $90,000 to the lender. The leveraged loss in this case is 200% ($20,000 loss divided by $10,000 cash investment = 200%), compared to an all-cash purchase loss of 20% ($20,000 loss divided by $100,000 cash investment = 20%). Again, sales costs and loan pay down are not included, to simplify the numbers.

◆ ◆ ◆

Essential Takeaway

> **Essential Takeaway:** *For small investors leverage offers the best tool for a big profit from a small stake. The essential strategy is to buy wisely and reach for the largest loan you can, given your situation. The secret is to rely on your team of professionals to help you find, analyze, purchase and manage a property to minimize your risk and maximize the possible returns from leverage.*

◆ ◆ ◆

---

2. Income From Positive Cash Flow[††]

The positive cash-flow strategy is particularly attractive to investors with a goal of long-term income and cash to invest in the purchase, either from outside income (salaries, etc.) or surplus income from other rental properties. In today's market, the convergence of lower prices, low interest rates and high renter demand can make the cash flow strategy a winner.

> ### [††]*Positive Cash Flow*
> Quite simply, positive cash flow is having more rent coming in than you pay out in expenses. Cash flow before tax is the difference between rents (income) and costs (loan payments and operating expenses). Subtract expenses from income and if you have money left over, that's positive cash flow. If you have to "feed" the property meter — put money from your pocket toward paying the expenses — you have negative cash flow.

Before or after taxes? Smart investors know the difference that depreciation[††] makes and how it can turn a negative cash flow before taxes into a positive cash flow after taxes. The ideal situation for many investors is to have positive cash flow before taxes. Perhaps you made a large down payment that kept mortgage payments less than your rental revenue. Or, you held the rental long enough for once upside-down rents to increase to become a positive cash flow. Then again, maybe you rehabbed the property to command a higher rent. Whatever the case, many investors find pretax positive cash flow a smart strategy to produce current income.

††*Depreciation*

Depreciation is unquestionably the most important tax incentive for investment properties. Simply, Uncle Sam assumes that a building and improvements "wear out" over time and become worthless. But land never wears out.

That's why it's essential to know that the land's value must be subtracted from your purchase price to establish your "depreciable base" for tax purposes. Depreciation "losses" are deductible from income, when in fact the property may be increasing in value. Accountants call depreciation the "write-off for obsolescence."

Much more on depreciation shortly.

3. Tax Advantages Turn Negative Cash Flow To Positive.

If rents break even with expenses or you can tolerate feeding a property with cash out-of-pocket, a range of tax deductions can convert a negative pretax cash-flow property into a shelter for other income. (Keep in mind, this is not a tax-help book — seek out professional advice for your particular tax situation.) Not uncommonly, even with a positive cash-flow property, a temporary negative cash flow can be caused by a tenant vacancy or major repair. On the bright side a well-maintained property has the best chance to grow in value over time.

Essential tax facts for investors. If you've purchased a home as an investment, you can reduce your taxable rental income by deducting rental-related expenses at least up to the income from the property. Deductions include expenses from interest to insurance and from maintenance to the Big D: Depreciation. Almost every dollar you spend on your investment property is tax deductible, within certain limits. Here are some examples (not all will apply):

- ▶ **Mortgage, taxes and fees:** Monthly mortgage payment of principal and interest, real estate taxes, personal property taxes, local county taxes, sales taxes, business license fees, homeowner's association or condo/coop fees, etc.
- ▶ **Insurance:** Hazard, general liability, "loss of rent," tenant relocation, credit life, flood, bonding, etc.
- ▶ **Services:** Trash collection, pest control, lawn service, furnace/AC tune-up, housekeeping, memberships, renting furniture, equipment or appliances, etc.

▶ **Utilities (not paid by tenant):** Electric, gas, water, sewer, Internet, cable/satellite TV, etc.

▶ **Maintenance:** Carpet cleaning; carpentry; repairs for appliances, HVAC, electrical and plumbing; painting; cleaning; and supplies.

▶ **Improvements:** Major projects, such as new roof, kitchen rehab, bath remodel, water heater or furnace/AC replacement, etc.

▶ **Professional services:** Accountant (tax filing, bookkeeping, depreciation, reports), attorney (lease review, eviction, advice), property manager, etc.

▶ **Administrative services:** Advertising, travel, office supplies, etc.

Two important *exceptions* to the "everything is deductible" rule: (1) The portion of your monthly payment that goes toward reducing your loan balance ("principal payment"), and (2) cash outlays for capital improvements to the property that must be depreciated.

In addition, when you sell a business property, some or all the profits you realize may qualify for long-term capital gains, which are taxed at a much lower rate than ordinary income.

Smart Tip: Get professional tax help. Tax laws change constantly, and today's laws are almost mind boggling in their complexity. Plus, tax laws are different in each state and sometimes even among municipal jurisdictions. There's simply no substitute for sound, professional advice from a tax expert familiar with your situation and investment.

More deduction limits: What you might not know is that you may be able to deduct up to $25,000 in losses from your rental real estate against income from other sources. Here's how you qualify, according to tax forms from the IRS *(http://www.IRS.gov)*:

💬 Your Adjusted Gross Income (AGI) must be $100,000 or less (not counting any loss from "passive activities") and after allowable adjustments to AGI or taxable Social Security benefits. If your AGI is between $100,000 and $150,000, you may be able to deduct some or all of your losses from rental real estate, depending on the amount of the loss.

💬 You must own at least 10% of the property and "actively participate" in its management. (If you chose the tenants and approved maintenance outlays, for example, that's considered "active" participation.)

💬 If losses from rental property were suspended in prior years, they are fully deductible in the year the property is sold.

📭 Want to learn more? Check out IRS Publication 527, *Residential Rental Property* (Including Rental of Vacation Homes) and consult your tax professional.

Everything You Need To Know About Depreciation	Beyond the tax deductions allowed for operating expenses and property taxes, a huge advantage for investors can be summed up in one word: Depreciation. The depreciation deduction alone can sometimes turn a property's negative cash flow positive.

Rabbit Or Tortoise: Which Depreciation Is Best?	Ask your tax advisor. Sheltering outside income or producing positive cash flow are two criteria that will help you decide. If your tax advisor says, "You've got a problem. Your property is producing

taxable income," that's a nice problem to have. Maybe it's time to buy another property or increase your depreciation deduction and shelter the income. Until then, you'll need to decide which of two depreciation methods is ideal for your situation: straight-line depreciation or accelerated depreciation.

Straight line to depreciation deductions. Uncle Sam allows you to deduct depreciation based on a 40-year useful life of the improvements (sales price – land value = depreciable base improvements). It's also called the Alternative Depreciation System (ADS). Once you elect straight-line depreciation, you can never revoke it. For example, if your $100,000 property is valued at $70,000 for the building and $30,000 for the land, using the 40-year "straight-line method" gives you an annual depreciation of $1,750 ($70,000 divided by 40 = $1,750). Depreciation is a "non-cash expense" requiring no actual payment of money out-of-pocket. The depreciation amount is added to the deductible expenses and subtracted from taxable income.

Here's an example:

▶ Annual rental income ($500 x 12): $6,000

Less:

▶ Operating expenses: $600
▶ Property taxes: $1,400

► Mortgage interest: $4,000
► Depreciation: $1,750
Sub-total annual costs: $7,750
► Taxable income (loss): ($1,750) [$6,000 – $7,750 = $1,750 loss]

Since you are at least a 10% owner of the property and actively participate in the operations of the property, the loss of $1,750 can be deducted from your outside income, thus reducing your taxable income and your taxes. For an investor in the 28% tax bracket, this deduction is a tax savings of $490 ($1,750 x .28 = $490). (For simplicity, these figures do not reflect the possibility that a lower taxable income might put you in a lower tax bracket, which would reduce your savings.)

Accelerated depreciation makes a good thing better. If you think straight-line depreciation is cool, just wait to you see what accelerated depreciation can do for your bottom line.

To stimulate real estate investment, Uncle Sam's Modified Accelerated Cost Recovery System (MACRS) allows investors to speed up the depreciation process in the first years a property is put into service using the General Depreciation System (GDS). These GDS rules allow you to shelter an even greater amount of income. (Just another way investors get richer while tenants pay their mortgage.)

In a nutshell, GDS allows investors to divide the property basis by 27.5 years to produce an accelerated-declining-balance depreciation figure (about 3.64% per year compared to 2.5% ADS) that in our example produces an accelerated depreciation for the first year of $2,545 ($70,000/27.5 = $2,545). The tricky part is that accelerated depreciation is subtracted from a lower depreciated base in subsequent years. This lower base ("declining balance") produces a lower accelerated depreciation every year after that. Quite simply: Your property will become "worthless" from a depreciation standpoint well before 27.5 years — and your invaluable tax deduction will stop (assuming you don't "over depreciate" and make Mistake #1: Deducting too much depreciation. More shortly.)

Here's an example:
► Annual rental income ($500 x 12): $6,000
Less:
► Operating expenses: $600
► Property taxes: $1,400

► Mortgage interest: $4,000
► Accelerated depreciation (first year): $2,545
Sub-total annual costs: $8,545
► Taxable income (loss): ($2,545) [$6,000 – $8,545 = $2,545 loss first year]

———— ◆ ◆ ◆ ————

Essential Takeaway

Essential Takeaway: *Taking depreciation on property — whether rental property, a principal residence or a second home — increases your capital gain (and therefore tax liability) upon sale. Your tax advisor will tell you that your ultimate tax liability must be weighed against the cash flow advantages on current income. Loosely translated: How ya gonna pay your bills today while you wait for years to sell the place? Tax treatment of depreciation claimed on real property varies depending on whether depreciation was taken before or after May 6, 1997. For detailed information, consult IRS Publication 523* Selling Your Home *(http://www.IRS.gov).*

———— ◆ ◆ ◆ ————

Costly Depreciation Mistakes To Avoid

Mistake #1: Deducting too much depreciation.

Rookie investors (or those without a smart accountant) may meet a nasty surprise when they sell their property because they don't know Uncle Sam always gets his taxes in the end. This is called "recapture of excess accelerated depreciation." Uncle Sam totals the accumulated depreciation deductions and subtracts from the original property cost ("basis"). If we assume you sell the property for a profit, your gain is increased by using the lower property cost basis. The effect increased your taxable gain from the sale . . . and that increases your capital gains tax liability. In the situation where the accelerated depreciation is greater than the straight-line depreciation figure, then the "excess depreciation" is taxed as ordinary income, just like your salary. Double ouch!

TOOLKIT

Solution: If you hold the property long enough to qualify, most or all of your gains will be subject to the lower long-term-gains tax rate. Smart investors track their depreciation deductions carefully and consult with their tax advisor. One choice is to stop taking accelerated depreciation deductions once you hit the straight-line max. Another choice is to cash out—a number of ways are available—to take your profits. (More on cashing out in the last chapter.) Bottom line: Taxes are "deferred" through depreciation deductions, not forgotten. Uncle Sam will collect those taxes at sale time.

Mistake #2: Confusing personal property with real property

Personal property, such as refrigerators, clothes dryers, washing machines, window air conditioners, ovens and ceiling fans, often convey with the sale but are not *real property* because they are not permanently attached. Compared to real property, personal property wears out faster ("shorter useful life"). For depreciation purposes, personal property items can be deducted separately in proportionately larger annual amounts than real estate. Confusing these separate depreciations will muddle your tax calculations.

Solution: Personal property should be depreciated on a separate schedule, not lumped into the depreciation schedule with real property. Keeping it separate allows you to reap tax breaks from the deductions as non-cash expenses. Remember to treat personal property deductions separate from real property depreciation at the time of sale to reckon your gains with the Tax Man.

Mistake #3: Not investigating your local assessor's improvement ratio.

Inexperienced investors sometimes estimate the portion of a property's value that is attributed to land and to improvements using an estimate of 20% land and 80% buildings and landscaping. This figure is called the "improvement ratio." Unfortunately, using a ballpark or best guess can get you in hot water with local taxing authorities.

Solution: Check with the local tax assessors' office and get their official ratio. By using the official improvement ratio in the property's jurisdiction to calculate your depreciation deductions, you can maximize the depreciable base . . . and also your tax breaks.

Mistake #4: Assuming the depreciable base is simply the sales price.

Solution: The tax code requires you add in other acquisition costs to the sales price to determine your base, such as transfer taxes, closing charges, lawyer's fees, title search, survey and other acquisition expenses. These costs increase your depreciable base and your tax savings. The cost of improvements you make to the property increase your base even more.

Mistake #5: Blithely continuing the depreciation schedule of the previous owner.

Solution: Whatever you do, don't pick up on depreciation where the previous owner left off. Every new owner begins at zero, as if the property had never been depreciated. You can depreciate the property on the new cost basis established by the "useful life" set by tax rules in effect at purchase and then calculate your straight-line or accelerated depreciation deductions.

4. Appreciation Builds Wealth Quietly.

We've all heard the investment mantra: Buy low, sell high. Appreciation is the principle behind this wealth builder as the property increases in value over time. In simple terms, profit is appreciation minus expenses. While depreciation reduces taxes, appreciation is how real estate increases in value . . . and ultimately beats inflation.

No one can be absolutely certain whether a property will increase or decrease in value. Yet one stunning fact is clear: Throughout the valuation cycles of the last hundred years, there were times when market corrections reset values lower after a period of growth. Think the Great Depression of the 1930s and the Great Recession of the 2000s. Experienced investors know the period just after a reset offers some of the best opportunities to buy low . . . then hold and sell high later, when natural demand and inflation eventually push values higher again.

Smart investors know inflation and appreciation won't make you rich quickly. But appreciation can make you rich steadily. If you don't want to wait for prices to escalate, consider another strategy. Renovate the property in a way that minimizes expense but maximizes your ability to charge higher rents. Put another way: Renovation can create price appreciation beyond inflation.

◆ ◆ ◆

> **Essential Takeaway:** *Not every property is a suitable rental, partly because the location or condition doesn't offer appreciation potential. Determining if a property is an ideal rental is only rewarded by fast action. More on analyzing and "running the numbers" on potential properties in Chapter 4: ANALYZE.*

◆ ◆ ◆

5. Take Profits From Equity Buildup When Time Is Right.

Last but not least, equity buildup—the difference between the property value and the outstanding loan balance—is the fifth way to profit from investment real estate. As we saw in tool #4, appreciation is one way your equity grows. Also, improvements ("sweat equity") may increase your equity. Additionally, mortgage principal payoff also grows your nest egg. In a nutshell, renters pay your mortgage every month—another example of using OPM to build wealth. In the case of a $100,000 property financed with 10% down and a $90,000 loan that appreciates from $100,000 to $120,000 in value, appreciation built equity to $30,000 ($120,000 less $90,000 = $30,000). It gets better: Over time, the monthly rent payments reduce that $90,000 loan principal to $80,000. Now your equity is $40,000 ($120,000 less $80,000 = $40,000).

Equity buildup is often referred to as "shadow income" because it's only realized when refinancing or selling. The combination of appreciation *and* principal paydown allows you to set an "equity target" that can trigger the day when it's time to cash out. Smart ways to cash out on this equity are detailed in Chapter 7: CASH OUT.

OK, Smartie. So much for the nitty gritty of essential investing tools you'll need. Onward to the fun part! In the next chapter, we'll drill into proven ways to find wealth-building investment properties . . . and how to avoid the costly mistakes of money pits among other land mines.

Chapter 2 Roundup

Smart Essentials TOOLKIT :: What You Have Learned

▶▶ 5 essential tools every investor needs.

▶▶ How leverage works and how much is just right.

▶▶ Avoid the costly mistake of negative leverage.

▶▶ Enjoy lifetime income from positive cash flow.

▶▶ How tax advantages turn negative cash flow into positive.

▶▶ Everything you need to know about depreciation.

▶▶ Costly depreciation mistakes to avoid.

▶▶ How appreciation builds wealth quietly.

▶▶ Take profits from equity buildup when time is right.

Smart Essentials

Page	Essential Note

PROPERTIES

In this chapter, you'll learn smart ways to:

1. Find promising rental properties for sale.

2. Analyze the profit potential of every property by the numbers.

3. Evaluate the right market value before you make an offer to buy.

PUT GOOD INVESTMENTS BEFORE GOOD TAX SHELTERS

Finding a good rental property in a good rental neighborhood at a good price with good investor financing—regardless of the tax consequences or any tax code changes—is essential to profiting from the investment. As they say: The simplest strategy is to buy low and rent high. The idea, of course, is to let a tenant's rent pay your mortgage. Tax consequences are significant but secondary.

> **Defining your investment strategy comes first:**

- ▶ Do you want "ugly properties" to fix up and turn over?
- ▶ Do you plan to hold for a time then sell or refinance?
- ▶ Do you plan to hold indefinitely for income—what investors call "patient money"?
- ▶ Do you want to buy distressed, below-market foreclosures, auctions or short-sale properties?
- ▶ Do you want to buy starter homes or condos?
- ▶ Does your strategy call for investing in a specific area or low-down-payment properties?
- ▶ Do you want to target "rent-to-own" properties where your tenant-buyer signs a lease with an option to purchase, then cares for the property and pays rent on time like it's their own?

The conditions on the ground will determine whether one strategy profits while another doesn't pay. Quite simply, putting taxes, cash flow and accounting techniques aside for the moment, you want to select properties that make money *both when you buy* and *when you sell.* That means: (1) buying rentable properties for the best possible price, and (2) choosing properties that will increase in value through upgrades and appreciation over time.

Finding Promising Properties Takes Homework

Serious investors use a top real estate agent who specializes in finding income properties. Why? It doesn't cost the investor anything—typically the property seller pays the commission for both the listing and buying agents. A creative agent is worth a king's ransom. Share your goals and strategies and turn the agent loose to scour the market for you. (More on buying and financing strategies in Chapter 4: ANALYZE.)

That said, nothing proves more valuable than taking a discerning look at the property yourself—time to throw on the coveralls for your initial inspection.

So where do you look and what do you look for? The first place to look is your own stomping grounds. You know the area best, and you can "keep an eye" on a property easily if you live nearby. Just remember: You are investing in *rental property* not an owner's residence. Often this means not looking in the "best" part of town (nor in the "worst" area either). Specializing in one area has the double advantage of being able to use the same network of local advisors—real estate agent, property manager, handyman, inspectors, etc.

Search areas that have been consistently popular with renters in the past—areas near public transportation, employment centers, shopping, good schools and/or colleges, recreational opportunities, etc. You want tenants who *need* to rent. Renters who can afford high rents will turn over quickly because they can afford to buy. In your search, consider doing a "Location Study" with careful input from your investment agent.

Gather statistics using tax records such as percentage of owner-occupied homes compared to rentals, average property age, tax assessments, area rent trends using rent per square foot or rent per bedroom factors, vacancy rates (if available) and appreciation history. This research takes the guesswork out of your figures. The statistics arm you with vital information on which property types rent quickly and longer so you're not wasting your time on unpopular investment duds.

CHAPTER 3

PROPERTIES

Give particular attention to condominiums versus townhomes versus single-family homes. While one rental property type booms in one area, in another area renters may prefer a different type of property. *Smart Tip:* Establish the maximum monthly "negative" cash flow you can tolerate given your outside income. Use this threshold-of-pain limit to guide you away from higher prices and costlier housing types.

Condo caution: Beginning investors often start with condos. Although condos can be attractive, especially for price-to-rent ratios, your investment return at condo resale will be greatly affected by the actions of others beyond your control. The attractiveness and value of condos can be impacted by good or bad condo management, selloff by other owners, multiple competing units that are similar if not identical, high percent of unsold units, vacancies or foreclosures throughout the complex, developer bankruptcy—just to name a few disasters.

Fixer-upper caution: Buy low, rent high. Who can beat a fixer-upper? Remember: Investor specials take money to make money. Fixer-uppers often need more than paint and carpet. These temptations come in many varieties from for-sale-by-owner properties (FSBOs) to foreclosures; from unmaintained rentals to vacant/abandoned properties. Maximize your profits by remembering these tips:

- ▶ Try to pay wholesale, not retail. Stop when you hit your price ceiling; avoid getting caught up in a bidding war.
- ▶ Plan extra cash for fix-ups. Get itemized estimates so repairs don't cost twice as much as planned—or take twice as long.
- ▶ Get clear title—requires a title search and payment for insurance.
- ▶ Analyze cash flow. Avoid paying out more than rent checks can cover.
- ▶ Increase property value. Repair small problems before they become big ones down the road. There's a big difference between a "handyman's special" and a "money pit."

If you want to build sweat equity, hire a professional inspector to ensure that refurbishing the property won't cost a fortune. Expect to receive thorough reports on the home's condition, then get estimates from your general contractor for repairs or improvements required to rent out the house. Take into consideration any required local-government inspections and upgrade requirements for rental properties.

◆ ◆ ◆

> **Essential Takeaway**

> **Essential Takeaway:** *Don't be put off by a property in bad cosmetic condition if it has good bones and is structurally sound. Often a low sales price may reflect a bad impression from cosmetic flaws that can easily be fixed — that's a true bargain property!*

◆ ◆ ◆

9 Smart Ways To Find Promising Properties

1. Look for broad rental appeal, which will also attract the widest range of future prospective buyers.

2. Specialize in one property type, whether single-family houses, townhouses, condominiums, "plexes" with duplexes, tris or quads, or small apartment buildings with separate electric meters. (Owning several units allows you to spread costs and vacancies over multiple properties.) You might even occupy one of the units yourself. Keep in mind that single-family houses traditionally have the greatest resale market.

3. Become a student of sales prices of similar properties in the area to build your sense of market value.

4. Look for a neighborhood with a low crime rate and where nearby properties are well-maintained.

5. Look for property with maintenance or improvement needs that you're sure you can handle. A good start: Solid construction and major systems in good condition.

6. Watch for sellers less interested in getting the max price than they are in just getting out of the property. These sellers include: (1) Investors who have depreciated a rental to the max, (2) investors who face emergency cash needs, (3) distressed owners facing foreclosure, and (4) estate sales.

7. Compare rents for similar units nearby. One handy rule-of-thumb is rental rate per bedroom (rent divided by bedrooms = rent per bedroom). New investors are often surprised at the small range between low and high rental rates for similar-size units in a community.

8. Concentrate your search for rental properties in the relatively lower price ranges that can be supported with rents.

9. Visit open houses, drive through areas, inspect properties, compare listings online, talk with your mentor or other investors, and run the numbers with property-analysis software.

Top 10 Property-Finding Mistakes To Avoid

Mistake #1: Don't buy a property if you won't have enough income from rents and other sources to cover the mortgage payments and taxes as well as emergency repairs or extra vacancies that reduce income.

Mistake #2: Don't finance with an adjustable-rate loan or balloon payment unless you are sure you can make larger mortgage payments (after rate adjustments) or come up with the lump sum when it's due — or that you'll be able to refinance as needed.

Mistake #3: Don't base your offer price on a multiple of rental income, such as 8 times annual rent or 100 times monthly rent — these quickie formulas rarely fit a property or a market, making them unreliable. The sales prices of local comparable properties offer the best gauge of value.

Mistake #4: Don't buy unless you've put together before-tax and after-tax cash-flow statements with verified figures.

Mistake #5: Don't invest in properties with delayed maintenance issues and where the seller's income and expense statements show an unrepresentative positive picture, unless the price is discounted to compensate for rehab costs.

Mistake #6: Don't buy in a community where most of the people work for the same employer. Unexpected cutbacks and closings could reduce property values or increase vacancies.

Mistake #7: Don't accept a contract until everything you and the seller have agreed upon is in writing.

Mistake #8: Don't ask how much a property will appreciate; ask yourself what appreciation rate you are comfortable with and look for supporting evidence that the property will increase at that rate.

Mistake #9: Don't forget to examine existing leases, especially for end dates and renewal rental rates. Make sure the seller turns over renters' security deposits at settlement.

Mistake #10: Don't make a down payment so small that you are left with a negative cash flow after taxes—especially if your outside income isn't large enough to allow you to "feed the meter" of extra costs.

All Things Equal, Which Is The Smarter Property Buy?

Picture two promising properties: Both require the same cash investment, both generate the same cash flow, both have an identical projected future sale price. Which one is the better investment? Although some analysis is more art than science, the more you can quantify your risks, the more winners you'll pluck from the lake of losers.

● **Vacancies matter.** Buy the property that rents fastest. Check out vacancy rates in the area. Ask how long properties stay on the rental market. Look for the type of properties that rent best. In some areas, condos, townhouses or multi-family units may be easier to rent than single-family homes. In other areas, the reverse may be true.

● **Age matters.** Older properties cost more to maintain. Over the years, higher expenses produce lower cash flows. It's better to buy the newer property or the one that's already in good shape and easy to maintain. Avoid properties that need expensive repairs or replacements, which can seriously impact the profitability of your investment. Since investment homes are often sold "as is"—meaning you, the new owner, will be responsible for bringing the property up to standards for rentals in the area—you can minimize your financial outlay by selecting a property that does not require extensive structural repairs or major improvements.

● **Proximity matters.** Choose nearby properties vs. those far away. Shop close to home. Even if you hire someone to manage the property for you, chances are you'll need to visit occasionally. *Smart Tip:* Think twice before putting "all your eggs in one basket." Although managing a property is easier if it's closer to home, buying in different neighborhoods diversifies your portfolio. Having investments in different areas allows you to benefit if one market appreciates rapidly, but also gives you some protection should one market depreciate.

● **Resale matters.** Prefer the property with the best resale potential. Look to the future. Find out from your agent and other investors/ landlords what is predicted for the area's rental market in years to come.

PROPERTIES

Learn what plans are underway to change the neighborhood (e.g., road construction, new homes) that might affect the value or demand for your investment.

● **Turnover matters.** High-turnover areas may indicate rental neighborhoods, which typically appreciate more slowly than owner-occupied homes . . . and sometimes depreciate. Prefer the property in the more stable neighborhood among owner-occupied homes where rentals are permitted.

Get Smart About Legal Issues

Be sure local zoning ordinances and homeowners association rules allow you to rent out the property as you envision. Seek information about rental restrictions that may affect how long or how often the property may be rented and the number of occupants allowed.

Although federal laws generally apply to discrimination and your responsibilities with respect to environmental health hazards, including lead paint and asbestos, the landlord-tenant relationship is governed by federal, state *and* local laws.

States laws may address discrimination and environmental issues as well as security deposits, housing standards, right of entry, eviction procedures, maintenance and repairs, and other rental rules. Local ordinances may regulate rent amounts and the frequency and amount of rent increases, among other matters.

A local investor-specialist agent will know — or know how to find out — about applicable laws in the area being considered, particularly regarding rent control, max occupancy, parking, tenants' rights (eviction, right of first refusal to purchase, etc.). Check out these sources:

▶ Your state housing-services or consumer-affairs office.

▶ Local landlords' organizations.

▶ Your landlord-tenant law attorney.

Avoid These Costly Property-Selection Mistakes

As with any investment, rewards also carry risks. Understanding those risks — and smartly moving to avoid them — is the best blueprint for success.

Mistake #1: Buying in an area where property values show signs of declining. Property values in any market can take a hit from a recession in the local economy to a sudden change of character in the neighborhood. Also, your profit can be crushed by an unexpected repair expense, prolonged vacancy or a sudden need for cash that could force you to sell early.

Solution: Be aware of the risks and minimize the pitfalls by buying smartly. As they say, knowledge is the best solution. One of your best resources is a star real estate agent who specializes in working with investors. They make it their business to constantly sweep the property listings and their own network of contacts to uncover promising rental properties for sale. Bar none: Inside, local smarts are unbeatable.

Mistake #2: Being beaten to the best properties by other investors. Let's face it: There are more amateurs in every market than there are savvy investors. Yet competition is fierce for the best properties, good tenants and qualified buyers.

Solution: Knowing when to buy — and knowing when to pass on a property — is essential. Good properties don't last long in today's rental market. That's why the smartest investors have their funds or financing lined up and their team of advisors at the ready; they recognize the importance of decisive action when an opportunity emerges.

Mistake #3: Buying a property only because its price is low. Just because the property is inexpensive doesn't make it a great investment. If the property does not fit the needs of your target renters (read: stable, reliable), you'll be unlikely to rent the property continuously and effectively and will likely lose money in the long term.

Mistake #4: Buying a property that's hard to keep rented. Empty equals money lost. If your renters turn over quickly, leaving gaps of time with the property unrented, you're unlikely to meet your investment goals. Check on the property's rental history and examine the amenities around the home, including proximity to transportation, shopping and workplaces, as well as the quality of the schools.

Mistake #5: Not understanding your costs. When you start investing in real estate, you need to know exactly how much money you can afford for closing costs, fix-up and maintenance, taxes and general holding costs. Be prepared for unexpected repair expenses, for problem tenants, for remodeling that uncovers more issues that need fixing, and for big-ticket items that may need replacing on short notice.

Mistake #6: Expecting it to be easy. Owning your own home is one thing. Owning an investment property is completely different. Besides having to adhere to local laws for landlords, you may eventually find it easier to hire a property manager, which could soak up around 3% to 15% of the monthly rent. If your profit margins look thin, reconsider your investment.

Beware of profit-killing gotchas. Finding promising properties is one thing. Pulling the trigger to buy is another. You'll learn plenty about analyzing properties in the next chapter.

Chapter 3 Roundup

**Smart Essentials PROPERTIES ::
What You Have Learned**

▶▶ Good properties are good investments before being good tax shelters.

▶▶ 9 smart ways to find promising properties.

▶▶ Top 10 property-finding mistakes to avoid.

▶▶ All things equal: Which is the smarter property to buy?

▶▶ Get smart about legal issues.

▶▶ Avoid six costly property-selection mistakes.

Smart Essentials

Page	Essential Note

ANALYZE

In this chapter, you'll learn smart ways to:

1. Analyze a good deal when you first find one.

2. Use insider techniques to size up the profit potential of any property.

3. Know how to evaluate the real numbers before making an offer.

ANALYZE A GOOD DEAL WHEN YOU FIRST FIND ONE

Return on your investment is calculated in two ways: positive cash flow and long-term appreciation. Ideally you can make money either way. In today's market, investors in many areas have seen prices stabilize and begin to climb, offering potential to make money on property resale. However, the primary return on your investment today is likely to be cash flow — not a quick resale.

Note there are two different questions: (1) What income can you expect? and (2) What rate of return on your cash investment will the property yield? Both answers are estimated as a dollar amount and a percentage. For cash flow, smart investors first look at "price-to-rent" ratios, then run the numbers for cash flow two ways — "before taxes" and "after taxes." For rate of return, one common analysis is called "cash on cash" that primarily uses price and a number of other key factors. Another bottom-line technique is analyzing the "internal rate of return" on the cash invested.

---

6 Essentials To Evaluate The True Numbers Smartly

● **Purchase costs.** If you don't already own the property, calculate how much money you need to invest in down payment and closing costs ("cash invested," "equity-cash investment"). Smart investors also include rehab costs to make a property rentable in their cash-to-be-invested figure.

● **Ownership costs.** As you budget, allow for operating expenses, such as principal, interest, escrows[††] for insurance and real estate taxes, maintenance and other operating expenses. (One rule of thumb pegs all costs at 33% of rental income.) Then add property-management fees (if any, typically 3%–15% of rents), plus utilities (if not paid by tenant) and income taxes. Make sure to set aside a reserve fund to cover unexpected repairs, and expect at least 1 to 3 months of vacancy between rental periods.

> ††*Escrows*
> Escrows are funds paid by the borrower each month, prorated to cover the quarterly, semi-annual or annual lump-sum payments due for taxes and hazard insurance. Expect your guesstimate to fluctuate over the years as rates change.

💬 **Financing costs.** Whether and how you finance the purchase — or pay all cash — will significantly affect your monthly payment. The size of your down payment is based on your credit rating, what you can afford and what loan program you use. If the property has been a rental, your mortgage lender may allow you to factor a portion of the property's average rental cash flow into your income to boost your borrowing power. That's even more likely if tenants are already in place with long-term leases.

💬 **Income.** You'll need to set a competitive rental price ("fair-market rent") and calculate your income with an assumption that you will have occasional vacancies between renters. To give you starter figures: Vacancy forecasts range from 7.5% (best case), 10% (expected), 12.5% (worst case). Keep in mind 1 month of vacancy = 8.3% lost income; two months = 16.7%; three months = 25% income lost for the year.

💬 **Taxes.** Factor tax breaks into your budget. Most property owners can take a tax deduction for mortgage interest, property taxes and a variety of other expenses, as well as depreciating the value of the property every year, as you learned in Chapter 2. For authoritative information on tax issues, see IRS Publication 527, *Residential Rental Property,* and consult your tax advisor.

💬 **Profitability.** If you purchase property to rent, it may take a few years before the profit rolls in. That doesn't necessarily mean it's a bad investment. By holding the property long enough, inflation may increase the rents you can charge, eventually generating enough income to exceed expenses. In addition, the best properties increase in value over time, rewarding owners with capital gains upon sale, especially if the

CHAPTER 4

ANALYZE

acquisition price was a bargain below market. Think of it this way: Do you consider your retirement fund a loss because you put money into it each month? No. You know that in the end, it will pay dividends and be profitable over time.

> **Four Insider Techniques To Size Up Every Property's Potential**

Investment properties are, after all, a business transaction. To make a sound business decision, you need to crunch the numbers. Essentially, investment calculations take two steps. First: The ballpark "initial analysis" that applies a rough calculation to put a property on your short list or chuck it into the passed-over pile. Second: A detailed "investment analysis" that requires detailed data and your key assumptions. This computerized result often defines your offer to purchase.

Third and fourth give you a more sophisticated "internal rate of return" and show you the dramatic impact of taxes on your cash flow. *Smart Tip:* Numerous excellent investment-property analysis software programs are available. Get one. Ask your agent, your accountant, property manager or other landlords about what they use. Here are the essential principles at play in analyzing any investment property.

> **Analysis Rule #1: Price-To-Rent**

As you shop, you'll want to ensure the rent you can charge will cover as much of your ownership costs as possible. Smart investors compare properties by looking at their "price-to-rent" ratios (P/R) as a first criterion (also, "gross rent multiplier" or GRM). Simply divide the listing price of the property by the annual rent you can expect to receive from it.

Example: Dividing the $100,000 price (our long-running example) by $10,800 in annual rent = 9.3 P/R ratio. Compare that to a similar-size property priced at $75,000 for the same $10,800 rent = 6.9 P/R ratio. The lower the number, the better the investment deal — assuming all other factors are equal.

You can also use the P/R ratio to flag the best areas to invest in, and to compare one metro market with another. Local figures are essential. Look for local data on average property prices and average rents to make your calculations. Moody's *http://www.Economy.com* regularly ranks 54 metro areas nationally by P/R ratio, and *http://www.Zillow.com*

offers "rent Zestimates" for specific properties. The best investment properties to buy often fall in the 10 to 15 price-to-rent range, which reflects relatively high rents and low property values.

Smart Tip: The price-to-rent ratio is a ballpark tool at best. Real bean counters use Capitalization Rate ("cap rate") as a more accurate valuation tool. Rather than gross rent, cap rate uses net operating income (NOI) after subtracting expenses and vacancy factors. Whatever formula you use, be careful to compare values for similar property types, and especially avoid comparing prices of rental homes to owner-occupied homes that reflect widely different underlying values. Closed sales prices, rather than listing prices, also increase accuracy.

Analysis Rule #2: Cash-On-Cash Return

A cash-on-cash (COC) return (also, "return on investment" or ROI) estimates your return on cash invested in the deal and is easy to calculate. Quite simply, a COC percentage is the property's annual net cash flow divided by your net investment. COC is a rough but useful back-of-the-envelope exercise in your toolkit. It's helpful because COC tells you how much cash your money is putting in your pocket.

Calculating Your Cash-On-Cash Return

25% Down Example: If you buy a $100,000 investment property with a $25,000 down payment, your mortgage is $75,000, at, say, 5% interest, with a principal and interest payment of $375 monthly. In addition you invest another 5% or $5,000 for closing costs, loan pre-paids and fix-up repairs. Your cash invested ("buyer's equity") starts at $30,000 ($25,000 + $5,000 = $30,000).

25% Down Cash-On-Cash Analysis

▶ Rent Monthly: $900
▶ Monthly Expenses: −$300 [33.3% of rent]
▶ Net Operating Income: $600
▶ Monthly Loan Payment: −$375
▶ Monthly Net Income: $225
▶ Annual Net Income: $2,700
▶ Cash Invested: $30,000

▶ Cash-On-Cash Return: 9% first year [$2,700 divided by $30,000 = .09]

Compare that to a savings account. You deposit money in the bank, and the bank pays you an annual return, say 1%. The 1% is the cash-on-cash return on your savings account. If you're comfortable with this 9% cash-on-cash return, then this could be a promising property. If not, walk away.

All Cash Example: Now let's look at a 100% example ("all cash") to buy the same property ($100,000 + $3,000 fix-ups = $103,000), thus producing significantly greater monthly cash flow.

100% Down Cash-on-Cash Analysis

▶ Rent Monthly: $900
▶ Monthly Expenses: –$300 [33.3% of rent]
▶ Net Operating Income: $600
▶ Monthly Loan Payment: –$0
▶ Monthly Net Income: $600
▶ Annual Net Income: $7,200
▶ Cash Invested: $103,000
▶ Cash-On-Cash Return: 7% first year [$7,200 divided by $103,000 = .07]

See the tradeoff? Annual income is much greater in this all-cash example ($7,200 versus $2,700), yet the 25% down example delivers a better first year COC return percentage (9% vs. 7%). All cash, of course, assumes you have the money, plus your cash risk is bigger in the all-cash example because your leverage ("other people's money") is smaller, in fact, zero.

Smart Tip: Although return on investment (ROI) and cash-on-cash (COC) return are basically the same, some investors also argue that return on equity (ROE) is the same analysis because the initial investment before you see any loan payoff or appreciation is equivalent to your cash investment (down payment). Close enough, but not exactly correct for two reasons.

First, your initial equity will be less than your cash investment because out-of-pocket closing costs, such as points, legal fees, and appraisal, are not included as part of your equity. That means your ROE will be higher than your COC return.

Second, if you buy below market value, your presumed equity from Day One will be higher than your cash investment and your ROE will be lower than your COC return. Remember, without a sale or professional appraisal, from a bank's viewpoint, your equity is technically based on your purchase price, not wishful resale thinking.

So much for quibbling.

◆ ◆ ◆

Essential Takeaway

Essential Takeaway: *As you analyze more properties, a sharp pencil will reveal what other investors have learned: Sought-after properties, like high-end or waterfront or fancy condos, generally have lower — or negative — cash-on-cash returns compared to moderately priced properties that offer higher positive cash flows. Go for the cash flow, not the prize properties.*

◆ ◆ ◆

Because cash goes in and cash comes out in many ways in real estate investments, a more sophisticated analysis than cash-on-cash is needed by smart investors. An "Internal Rate of Return" (IRR) calculates the true rate at which your real estate investment is increasing in value each year. Yet, remember that the exercise is based on assumptions that make the future figure squishy and perhaps of a more hypothetical than real value . . . unless the IRR benefits from investor/seller hindsight.

Analysis Rule #3: Internal Rate of Return

Internal Rate of Return (also, "annual percentage yield") is the total true return on your investment, taking into account depreciation, appreciation and equity gained from paying down the debt.

Smart Tip: The term "yield" is sometimes casually used to describe rent-less-taxes-and-insurance, which assumes no loan payment ("all cash"). The more-correct term than yield in this case is "cash flow before expenses." After expenses, the term is "net income." Figuring a true return is tricky because items such as the value of depreciation depend on the marginal tax bracket of your taxable income. You also have to make appreciation assumptions that will not be realized until the house actually sells. Only at sale do you make money or "monetize your amortization and appreciation," as bean counters say. That's one reason IRR is typically calculated over a holding period of 3 to 7 years, which is intentionally short because depreciation decreases with time.

Essential assumptions for 25% down example:

► Net Income: $225 monthly [$2,700 per year]

► Property Value: $100,000

► Initial Cash Investment: $30,000 [$25,000 down + $5,000 pre-paids and fix-up costs]

► Depreciation (first year): $2,900 [MACRS-GDS: $80,000 base divided by 27.5. Assume the property was put into service in January, thus qualifying for 12-month depreciation in the first year. Because the remaining depreciable property value declines every year, accelerated depreciation also declines every year.]

► Marginal Tax Bracket: 28% [28% and above makes real estate tax breaks most attractive]

► Appreciation: 6% that year [$6,000]

► Principal Paydown: $1,200 first year

Now let's run the following IRR:

► $2,700 Net Income

► $812 Depreciation Value [Tax saving: $2,900 depreciation x 28% tax bracket]

► $6,000 Appreciation [$100,000 x 6%]

► $1,200 Principal Paydown [$100 x 12 months]

► $10,712 Total Internal Return

► 36% Internal Rate of Return first year [$10,712 divided by $30,000 initial investment]

Keep in mind: Unlike cash-on-cash analysis, total internal return is not spendable cash. Appreciation was your biggest number, and it won't be realized until you sell the place. We've also assumed there are no deferred maintenance issues and that you are not going to sell the property at a loss.

Smart Tip: If you have a positive cash-on-cash return before taxes, your IRR percentage will always be an even better number.

◆ ◆ ◆

**Essential
Takeaway**

Essential Takeaway: *All forecasts are built on key assumptions: financing, rehab costs, rents, vacancies, depreciation rules and marginal tax rates, maintenance expenses, management fees, etc. If one or more assumptions prove wrong, the tables can easily turn. Expect high rents? Low vacancies? High tax breaks? Low expenses? Smart investors treat forecasts as a navigation chart to a destination. Along the way, they regularly check their position and make mid-course corrections to miss the icebergs that drift into their path.*

◆ ◆ ◆

**Analysis Rule #4:
Cash Flow Before
And After Taxes**

The most universal reckoning of success in investment properties, especially for hold-for-income landlords, is analysis of a property's cash flow before and after taxes. A greatly simplified example makes clear the impact of depreciation and other tax breaks on cash flow in a real estate investment.

Essential Assumptions:
▶ Cost of property: $100,000
▶ Cash Invested: $30,000 [$25,000 down + $5,000 closing and fix-up costs]
▶ Financing: $75,000 for 30 years at 5%; monthly principal and interest $375
▶ Monthly Rent: $900
▶ Annual Rent: $10,800
▶ Depreciable Base: $80,000 [Improvements (buildings, landscaping, etc.) assumed to be 80% of sale price.]
▶ Depreciation (first year): $2,900
▶ Marginal Tax Rate: 28%

CHAPTER 4

ANALYZE

Cash Flow Before Tax

All figures are annual for first year.

1. Annual Income: $7,200 [$10,800 rent – $3,600 expenses]

2. Principal: $1,300 [Paid principal ("amortization") is not a taxable expense, because payments increase your equity. Because it is a cash outlay, principal is an operating expense.]

3. Interest: $3,000

4. Taxes: $1,500

5. Insurance: $500 [All insurance, including hazard, liability, private mortgage insurance, credit life, credit disability, etc.]

6. Operating Expenses: $1,080 [10% annual rent example includes: accounting, leasing, and legal fees, property management, maintenance, repairs, services, supplies, miscellaneous, etc.]

7. Improvements: $1,080 [10% annual rent]

8. Reserve: $1,080 [10% annual rent for vacancy/non-payment losses and emergency repairs]

9. Annual Expenses Sub-Total: $9,540 [Add #2 through #8]

10. Cash Flow Before Tax: loss ($2,340) [$7,200 income (#1): $7,200 – $9,540 expenses (#9) = ($2,340) loss]

Return Before Tax: Loss (7.8%) [($2,340) negative cash flow before tax (#10) divided by $30,000 cash invested and multiply by 100.]

Cash Flow After Tax

Again, all figures are annual for first year.

11. Cash Flow Before Tax: ($2,340) loss

12. Principal: $1,300 [Removes principal, a cash outlay that is not taxable, from cash flow.]

13. Sub-Total: ($1,040) [($2,340) #11 – $1,300 #12]

14. Depreciation (1st year): $2,900 [MACRS-GDS: $80,000 base divided by 27.5]

15. Taxable Income (Loss): ($3,940) [($1,040) cash-flow-before-tax-less-principal (sub-total #13) + $2,900 depreciation (#14) to get total taxable income (loss) for first year. Result is a loss which shelters your personal income from other sources (#16).]

16. Tax Saving: $1,102 [$3,940 (#15) x .28%] [*Smart Tip:* Lowering your income may also lower your "marginal rate" tax bracket, thus reducing tax savings or tax liability. Some investors believe the cash-flow return before tax is a more realistic figure for this reason.]

17. Cash Flow Before Tax: ($2,340) [#11]

18. Cash Flow After Tax: ($1,238) [($2,340) before tax (#11) – $1,102 tax savings (#16)]

Return After Tax: Negative (4.1%) [($1,230) cash flow after tax (#18) divided by $30,000 cash invested and multiply by 100. Note: Depreciation deduction turned a negative cash flow into better return but still negative after tax.]

◆ ◆ ◆

Essential Takeaway

Essential Takeaway: *Smart investors know tax laws and financing options change rapidly, which is why having top-level advisors is essential to your success. Note that these hypothetical examples are for illustration and not intended as tax advice. You are strongly encouraged to seek professional consultation from your tax advisor.*

◆ ◆ ◆

Costly Analysis Mistakes To Avoid

Mistake #1: Thinking actual return at sale will reflect your pre-purchase WAG (wild-ass guess).

Solution: Once you've purchased and owned a property and the details are concrete, then a more sophisticated return on investment (ROI) analysis can be done. Because key assumptions from income to vacancies to expenses to future sale price are unknown until realized, a smart analysis can only be done with real-world numbers. (More on reaping your profits in Chapter 7: CASH OUT.) For now, run "What if...?" assumptions to shed light on key strategic questions:

▶ Which method of depreciation is best, straight-line or accelerated?

▶ If key income or expense factors are changed, how would the yield be affected?

▶ Would refinancing be advantageous, and how much?

▶ How long should you hold the property before putting it up for sale?

▶ Would an installment sale or cash payment produce the highest return?

Mistake #2: Buying only one property when you can afford two.

Solution: Imagine the dilemma of spending your cash to buy one higher-priced property or two less-costly ones. Smart investors know you're better off with the lower-priced properties, for example, buying two $100,000 townhomes rather than one $200,000 single-family house. Why? The impact of reserves for vacancies and improvements isn't as disastrous when you spread the cost among several properties. Simply put: If you have the cash to pay for two down payments, two closing costs and two rehab expenses, then the smartest strategy is to buy two properties not one.

Mistake #3: Investing in real estate for the sole purpose of tax-loss write-offs.

Solution: The purpose of real estate investing is not merely to produce large tax write-offs of expenses and to shelter other income. Smart investors know that big losses of many kinds can be deducted from their taxable income. If losses are what you want, you've got plenty of other choices, from gambling in Vegas to losing money at a business to financing Hollywood films to flushing cash into the latest mobile-app fad. The smart yardstick to bring to real estate investing is how to increase your wealth — not how to blow it.

Mistake #4: Not understanding the timing of your lifestyle and your goals.

Solution: During your working years, when you find your income exceeds your living costs, the time is right to save and invest that excess income. That's essential. Later, replacing your working income with investment and retirement income will allow you to retire. Even semi-retirement means filling the income gap with cash generated from savings. Understand that your real estate investment strategy may evolve from a negative "after-tax loss" goal while working to a positive "before-tax cash flow" in your retirement.

Mistake #5: Expecting to be a passive arm-chair real estate investor.

Solution: If you want to be an angel with no role but to supply cash, then being a limited partner is one option. But in today's market, if you want an investment that doesn't need much day-to-day attention, then real estate investing is probably not for you. Why? Real estate investments generally require involvement to some degree, even when professional managers watch over the performance of the investment. In the end, nothing replaces boots on the ground to select properties and know what needs to be done and when. Also, most investors learn that real estate requires decisions and actions on a continuing basis if they are to be productive.

You've done your homework. You've nailed your numbers. Now it's time to pull the trigger and buy that investment puppy. But just exactly how you craft an offer that leaves both sides satisfied is a balancing act (Chapter 5: PURCHASE). Let the games begin!

Chapter 4 Roundup

Smart Essentials ANALYSIS :: What You Have Learned

▶▶ Analyze a good deal when you first find one.
▶▶ 6 essentials to evaluate the true numbers smartly.
▶▶ 4 insider techniques to size up every property's potential:
  ▶ *Analysis rule #1:* Price-to-rent
  ▶ *Analysis rule #2:* Cash-on-cash return
  ▶ *Analysis rule #3:* Internal rate of return
  ▶ *Analysis rule #4:* Cash flow before and after taxes
▶▶ Costly analysis mistakes to avoid.

CHAPTER 5
PURCHASE

In this chapter, you'll learn smart ways to:

1. Shape a purchase offer to your advantage.

2. Use other people's money to get the best deal to fit your investment strategy.

3. Nail down the right financing that is critical to positive returns.

HOW TO CRAFT A PURCHASE OFFER TO YOUR ADVANTAGE

Smart investors go into negotiations with a "win-win" attitude. Your goal is for both the buyer and seller to get what they want—not to beat the seller down in defeat. Often the ability to compromise on one point to get another goes a long way. Smart investors stay focused on the cash a seller will receive rather than emphasize specific contract terms.

Smart Tip: Owner-occupant sellers, as compared to investor sellers, banks or institutions, may be more emotionally attached to their home and benefit from more-sensitive treatment. On the other hand, investor sellers are typically interested more in the numbers than the property. Adapt your negotiating approach to push your seller's hot buttons.

Just as the seller can accept, counter or reject your offer. You can also accept, counter or reject a seller's response. One effective negotiating technique is for your investor's agent to present your offer in several parts: (1) a "summary sheet" that shows the net cash to seller highlighted in a "bottom line"; (2) a "net sheet" that itemizes how the seller's net proceeds are calculated; and (3) the contract itself.

After back-and-forth and all points are agreed, you initial every counter, sign the contract and notify all principal parties. You will also submit a deposit check, or "earnest money," to show you are serious about completing the transaction.

Inside Tips On Contingencies And Investment Terms

All contracts differ, of course, but here are 10 key essentials to consider in every negotiation for income-producing real estate.

1. **Financing Contingency.** At the heart of your offer is financing. That's because how you pay for the purchase directly impacts the seller's walk-away cash and your investment return. Include specifics, such as total loan amount(s), loan term lengths or dates a second or third mortgage are due (if any), and the particular financing details (for example, down payment of $10,000 which is 10% of purchase price; first trust (mortgage) of $45,000 at 5% for 30 years; commercial second trust for $20,000 at 6% for 25 years; owner-held third trust for $25,000 at 6% interest only for 7 years).

2. **Inspection Contingency.** To be sure the property doesn't have structural or mechanical problems, make the contract contingent on you receiving a satisfactory building inspection report. Typically the buyer pays for this report. An inspection will either give you peace of mind that all is well or uncover needed repairs that can be negotiated with the seller — or prompt you to walk away.

3. **Property Management Contingency.** Consider making the contract contingent on the property being accepted by your professional property manager. Often a time limit is included such as 72 hours. This allows your property manager to determine if the property meets market standards and is acceptable for management.

4. **Earnest Deposit.** Indicate how much money you'll deposit to show your good faith, and also the additional amount you plan to add to make up your down payment. Some investors include proof of funds to reassure seller. This "earnest money" is deposited in escrow and returned to you if the sale does not go through and you have not defaulted on the contract.

5. **First Trust Balance.** Where the purchase involves a loan assumption of a first trust, include the exact amount of loan balance, interest rate and remaining loan term so all parties are clear.

6. **Rental Before Closing.** Consider a clause that gives you permission to advertise, show and line-up tenants before settlement. This provision gives you a 15- to 45-day lead time to screen a renter, and then begin your rental revenue as close to possession date as possible. Be careful not to lease property before settlement/closing.

7. **Closing Costs.** The custom of who pays closing fees varies by area, and also shifts between seller's markets and buyer's markets. Consult with your real estate agent and consider asking the seller to pay some or all the closing costs. Giving up this request later during negotiation can smooth acceptance of another point you want to insist upon.

8. **Walk Through.** Unless you agree to accept the property in "as is" condition, the seller is responsible for plumbing, heating, mechanical and electrical systems to be in working order at closing. Include a provision that gives you and/or your investor agent the right to a satisfactory "pre-closing walk-through inspection" no later than the day of closing.

9. **Personal Property.** Any items that would not cause damage if removed are considered personal property, not real property, and do not convey with the purchase unless itemized in the contract. Don't trust verbal agreements. Be sure to include specific items you want conveyed in the sale, such as washer, dryer, refrigerator, slide-in range, light fixtures, drapery rods, chandeliers or other items not physically attached.

10. **Assignment.** Here's where your mentor may come in. In the purchaser's line of the contract, you write "[Your Name] and/or Assigns." Also, include an addendum to the effect: "Seller also agrees this contract is contingent on approval by purchaser's partner." Your partner is your mentor with cash to buy. Together you'll agree on a relationship: Assign a portion or your entire interest to your partner, or you simply get a finder's fee from the closing proceeds, plus invaluable experience. Including another legal owner at settlement is convenient and less costly than re-recording the transaction later.

Each of these terms and contingencies will come with their own time frames so that inspectors or third-party persons can be included in the process.

FINANCE YOUR INVESTMENT WITH 'OTHER PEOPLE'S MONEY'

With today's interest rates and many attractive loan programs available on residential real estate, now may be the perfect time to buy an investment property. Be aware, though, lenders ask for larger down payments and charge somewhat higher interest rates for mortgages on non-owner-occupied properties. There's good reason.

Lenders consider investment property a higher risk than financing owner-occupied homes because investors have less to lose than walking away from a home they live in. There's also a greater risk the owner could default if the property sits vacant for a long period. Let's be honest: Owners who rely on rental income to make the monthly payment can quickly run into trouble. In addition, some renters don't care for properties as well as a live-in owner — which over time can erode the property's value.

10 Tips To Get The Best Mortgage Deal

Make sure your credit is in the best possible shape before making a loan application. In a nutshell: Your credit report and credit score decide your future.

Make yourself a financing expert. Other people's money is where you'll make or break your investment business. Know what options you have when it comes to financing the purchase, building or fixing up your rental property.

Find out what you can afford. Shop several lenders to determine how much cash you'll need to purchase, how much mortgage you qualify for and what type of loans make the most sense. Better yet: Get pre-approved for financing. Pre-approval means you have money ready to go and just need a property.

Ask whether the seller — or lender or government institution in a foreclosure — can provide your mortgage. If so, you may be able to get a lower down payment, a lower interest rate or easier terms.

Show the lender you can afford the payments without relying on rental income — or that you at least have enough cash reserves to weather several months of vacancy.

Make a sizeable down payment — more than the minimal 3.5% to 25% if possible. The more you have invested in the property, the less risky the loan looks from the lender's standpoint.

Demonstrate your ability to rent out the property by showing low local vacancy rates and proof that your rental amount is consistent with other rental properties in the area.

If the property has a consistent record of being rented, show that to the lender and let the lender know if you already have a tenant. The lender may consider a portion of the property's average rental income in the decision about how much to lend you.

● **Your lender will be particularly concerned** about a property's title being clear of any liens or other claims to ownership. Order a title search, or make sure the seller will deliver clear title, and ensure any issues are resolved before proceeding with the purchase.

● **Some lenders shy away from rehab loans** for fixer-upper properties or flipping because lenders don't like the added risk of a rehab job. In fact, if a "non-functional" property doesn't return an adequate appraisal upfront the lender may undervalue the property. That can mean you can't finance the purchase at all. Purchasing currently occupied properties may be a better bet.

How To Minimize Financing Costs On Investment Property

This section shares six smart strategies for using "other people's money" to pay purchase costs when you buy rental property. Choosing the "best" method depends as much on the circumstances of the investor as on the property and lender requirements. Numerous computer applications make it easy to compare terms and costs of a number of different loan structures. Ask your investment agent, accountant or mentor for recommendations.

◆ ◆ ◆

Essential Takeaway

Essential Takeaway: *We know the numbers in the following examples are not current — rates are always a moving target. What hasn't changed are the essential principles. We've also used round numbers because they illustrate the math simply . . . and make it simple for you to insert local figures and latest rates where needed.*

◆ ◆ ◆

● **Strategy #1: All cash.** For investors with deep pockets — or low-cost bargain properties — buying all cash maximizes your cash-flow income. Variations include a large down payment, say, 50% or more, that minimizes any mortgage expense for interest and principal. The NAR reports that nearly half of all investor buyers pay all cash. On a $100,000 property, the purchaser pays $100,000. No financing is required.

Benefits: Sellers know the deal will close smoothly and they will walk away with cash in hand. That confidence may make some sellers open to a price concession, where an offer from a buyer who needs financing may be less attractive even at full price.

● **Strategy #2: Self-financing.** Many investors get started by fixing up their primary residence to convert it into a rental. To move into the next property they self-finance the purchase with an equity loan or home-equity line of credit (HELOC). Equity financing means you have original cash equity, sweat equity and appreciation on your side. Self-financing and buy-fix-rent-buy-another is a time-honored strategy.

Benefits: Self-financing avoids applying to the bank for purchase financing. Ideally, positive cash flow pays down the credit line steadily to make new credit available for your next purchase.

● **Strategy #3: 10/90 Financing.** With a fixed rate mortgage, either conventional or government-backed, you borrow up to 90% of the purchase price at a flat interest rate for a fixed term, often 25 or 30 years. Your monthly principal and interest payments remain level throughout the mortgage (taxes, insurance and other fees can increase). You pay 10% down and finance 90% loan-to-value (LTV) with a commercial loan or assumption plus second trust.

Smart Tip: An assumption is when you take over the balance of an existing mortgage, either at the existing rate (which ideally is lower than current rates) or after renegotiating the terms of the loan with the lender. Assumptions are particularly common in the years following very low interest rates. Try to find lenders — or sellers — with assumable mortgage terms, not "due on sale" clauses.

Benefits: Investor pays 10% down and gets below market financing if assumption available. Seller gets cash from down payment and possible seller-held second trust. Also a lower down payment drives up your cash-on-cash return. Yet a low down payment (1) tends to carry a higher interest rate and (2) can cost you private mortgage insurance (PMI) to protect the lender from default if you have less skin in the game than 20%.

● **Strategy #4: FHA financing.** The Federal Housing Administration (FHA) offers special investor loans for up to 85% of the price or appraised value, whichever is lower. FHA doesn't actually make loans, rather it insures loans ("government-backed loans") which makes commercial lenders more willing to finance rental properties at lower interest rates and low down payment. When you put less than 20% down, FHA requires a Mortgage Insurance Premium (MIP) just like a conventional lender requires Private Mortgage Insurance (PMI). Some FHA loans require that the home must be owner occupied. That means FHA loans work for residential properties of 1–4 units where the investor lives in one of the units. Another scenario is to assume a current FHA loan where owners are not required to occupy the property.

Benefits: FHA investor financing is specifically tailored for investors, especially in today's market to encourage converting residential foreclosures into rentals. With this financing there is no need for a seller to take back a loan note and resales (not new construction) are typical.

● **Strategy #5: Adjustable-rate mortgage (ARM).** Doesn't that low rate sound great? Here's the catch: ARMs have a fixed repayment period, say 30 years, but the interest changes — and thus payments change — on a periodic schedule based on a particular interest index, such as Treasury Bills. ARMs usually have adjustment period and lifetime maximums ("caps") on rate increases and are best for investors seeking maximum income in the early years.

But ARMs aren't for everybody. The downside is that ARMs will adjust on a preset schedule, for example, payments are fixed for 1, 3, 5 or 7 years, then adjust annually for the remainder of the loan. The risk is rate/payment adjustments may cause higher expenses later without rents being able to keep up. Although maximum increases of interest and payment are capped for each adjustment period and also over the life of the loan, the unknown cost may not be acceptable for "buy and hold" strategies.

Benefits: In the first years, ARMs can produce maximum positive cash flow with low monthly loan payments, which can give you the highest possible income before taxes.

● **Strategy #6: Reverse mortgage.** If you are 62+ and have home equity, a don't-pay-till-later reverse mortgage is a consideration for investment property. Too good to be true? Almost. Compare costs carefully, and weigh taking money from an equity loan or cash-out refi instead. Fees for reverse mortgages can be buzz-killers. Upfront fees can include origination fees, points, mortgage insurance premiums (if FHA or equity drops below 20%), closing costs, servicing fees, and more. Interest is generally not deductible unless you make prepayments on the loan. Backend fees when you sell the house can also zap profits (assuming you care because you're not dead), such as admin fees or if the lender takes a share of the original equity at time of loan ("maturity fees") or the lender takes a share of the sale-price increase since the mortgage date ("appreciation fees").

Benefits: You don't make any monthly loan payments and there are no restrictions on how you spend the money. The loan is paid back when the house sells or the owner dies ("maturity event").

Essentials You Need To Know About Seller Financing

In today's market finding a seller willing to participate in seller financing may take some looking and convincing. Yet, if you find a seller with an assumable loan or who is interested more in income than cashing out, you may have found someone open to these strategies. Remember, the seller is under no obligation to sell to you. By making the deal attractive for the seller as well as the buyer ("win-win") investors can lock-in bigger returns in the future.

Smart Tip: The ideal seller is an investor who still wants income from the property but wants to be rid of active management and tenant issues. These "passive" owner/investors want loan payments more than rent payments and are willing to accept paper rather than cash.

🗩 **Seller Financing #1: 85/10/5 Financing:** With seller financing, the seller agrees to finance all or part of the purchase price at a reasonable interest rate for a relatively short time, say 5 to 7 years, with a "balloon" payment at the end. Seller financing can be negotiated in an almost endless variety of forms and terms, which can be advantageous to both you and the seller. In this example, the entire sale price is financed in three parts: You put in a 5% down payment. Seller finances 10% of the purchase with an owner-held second trust. A first mortgage with a loan-to-value (LTV) ratio of 85% is provided by a commercial loan. For sellers that want income more than cash, the proportion of the second and first trusts could be negotiated to, say, 60% / 35%.

Benefits: You pay only 5% down and seller gets that down-payment amount and first trust cash plus interest from the second trust.

🗩 **Seller Financing #2: Wraparound mortgage.** In wraparound ("wrap") financing, the lender (or seller acting as a lender) assumes the obligation of the existing mortgage and provides the buyer/investor with a new loan encompassing both the old balance and enough additional money to complete the purchase at the new sale price. From the seller's viewpoint, a wraparound is an alternative to a cash-out refinancing. The seller advances money that wraps the old loan balance plus an additional amount into a "new" loan at a rate above the existing rate but below prevailing interest rates. The loan term is the time left on the old mortgage. The seller continues to make the original payments to the commercial lender and receives larger payments from the investor. In general, only assumable loans are wrappable, often an FHA or VA loan that doesn't have a "due on sale" clause.

Benefits: Requires a small down payment and provides a lower monthly payment than a market-rate loan. The seller is no longer involved in property management or renter headaches. Plus, the seller leverages a lower interest rate into a higher yield for the seller. Caution: If market values decline and the investor defaults, the seller could foreclose and sell the property to pay off the mortgage. Be prepared to "sell" the owner on a wrap to allay any skepticism.

● **Seller Financing #3: Owner take-back.** Also, "deferred purchase money." Here the investor assumes the old loan, and the seller "takes back" some of the equity in the property through a second mortgage to the investor. If the investor agrees to a "balloon mortgage," then payments on the take-back are figured on a 30-year amortization but a balloon payment requires the investor to pay the balance of the loan after a shorter period, say 5 years. The investor will need cash to pay the balloon note or refinance or sell the property.

Benefits: Investor gets lower interest rate and lower monthly payments. Seller gets monthly income and down payment cash.

● **Seller Financing #4: 60/40 Refinance.** When a seller owns the property free and clear or has a low loan balance, a 60/40 refinance (or other proportional split of equity) can benefit both the seller and investor. The seller does a cash-out refinance of 60% of equity with new VA/FHA financing, and lends the remaining 40% in a seller take-back financing to the investor.

Benefits: Investor makes no down payment, and gets below-market financing. Seller gets cash from refinancing plus regular monthly income from the take-back note, possibly with a balloon payment.

● **Bonus Strategy: Partnerships.** Often, partnerships allow the small investor in on deals to buy multiple properties or larger commercial offerings using the pooled cash of the partner(s) in the same way that mutual funds invest in stocks, bonds and money markets. Partnerships run the gamut from private groups of a few investors to public partnership groups that raise huge capital pools sold to the general public.

In a private partnership, typically there is a "general partner" who is an individual or company, who manages the program in return for fees and a part of the profits. The other "hard money" investors who put up most of the cash are called "limited partners" because their liability for losses is limited to the amount they individually invest.

How the money works. Income from rent or mortgage payments is distributed proportionately to the limited partners. Also, partners can claim their share of certain expenses, such as interest on loans, property taxes and depreciation. After several years, say 7 to 12 years, a limited partnership may refinance or sell its properties and distribute any profits to the partners. Profits may receive favorable capital gains tax treatment but under certain circumstances can be subject to "recapture" which means profits could be taxed as ordinary income.

Costly Investor Financing Mistakes To Avoid

Mistake #1: Not studying all financing options that leap-frog lenders.

Solution: There are essentially three ways to avoid lender-financing for investment buyers:

1. Pay all cash. This strategy has the benefit of avoiding lender's red tape and consulting partners for every decision. The downside is you need to have the funds personally, and you're risking your money, not other people's money.

2. Use a line of credit from a local bank for down payment and rehab expenses. Rental income will repay the amount taken from the credit line, or you can repay the line when you sell. Both approaches leave your credit line available for additional investments.

3. Work with a partnership with one or more other investors. On the plus side, this strategy allows you to avoid investing all your resources and also shares the costs and expenses with your partners. This approach is especially common for larger commercial properties, but can work for single-family residential properties as long as you have a good working relationship with the partners.

Mistake #2: Being unprepared to qualify for lender financing.

Solution: In today's financing maze, there are five smart tips for success:

1. Make a sizable down payment. You'll get the best interest rate at 25% down or more if you can swing it.

2. Maximize your credit score. A FICO score below 740 can cost you in higher interest rates or require paying points to buy down the rate to be affordable. Check your credit early to be prepared.

3. Don't be afraid to ask owners if they would consider seller financing. With an uptick in motivated sellers wanting to get rid of their properties, more owners will consider helping you with the financing. Be sure to have a blueprint for the terms and figures you want.

4. Consider a private loan (also "hard money") from an individual who wants to own real estate but lacks time or know-how to find, purchase and manage property.

5. Don't say you'll live in the property when you won't. There are laws against illegal scams using "straw buyers." Avoid this costly mistake as it is fraudulent and could end up with you in jail.

◆ ◆ ◆

Essential Takeaway

Essential Takeaway: Regardless whether you invest individually or through a partnership, investors use financing to leverage the number or size of holdings or vary down payments to maximize cash flow; investors shelter income through depreciation deductions and tax breaks; and, all investors try to buy smart at a low price in hopes of selling later for a higher price through appreciation.

◆ ◆ ◆

Ultimately, you'll need to pull the trigger and buy. Investors that succumb to "analysis paralysis" and never jump in are lurkers, not investors. Knowing what to do once you actually buy a property is the subject of Chapter 6: MANAGE. Ready. Aim. Fire!

Chapter 5 Roundup

Smart Essentials PURCHASE ::
What You Have Learned

▶▶ How to craft a purchase offer to your advantage.

▶▶ Inside tips on contingencies and investment terms.

▶▶ Finance your investment with 'other people's money.'

▶▶ 10 tips to get the best mortgage deal.

▶▶ How to minimize financing costs on investment property.

▶▶ Essentials you need to know about seller financing.

▶▶ Costly investor financing mistakes to avoid.

CHAPTER 6

MANAGE

In this chapter, you will learn smart ways to:

1. Know what it takes to become a successful landlord.

2. Develop an iron-clad lease that meets your needs and property specifics.

3. Avoid costly property management mistakes common to rookie landlords.

KNOW WHAT IT TAKES TO BECOME A SUCCESSFUL LANDLORD

Managing your rental business is where you change hats from investor to landlord. Successful investors pull it off by focusing on three subjects: (1) Tenants, (2) Business and (3) Property Management.

The big question becomes: Do-it-yourself or hire professionals — or some combination in between?

Whatever you decide, you or someone must be available 24/7 for late-night emergency calls from tenants — or police. The property must at all times be "habitable," at least including safe and clean common areas (stairways, hallways, walkways); properly running systems (electrical, plumbing, sanitary, heating, ventilating, air conditioning); running water, hot water and heat in reasonable amounts and times; trash bins and removal.

Get On The Right Side Of The Law

As a landlord you'll be responsible to follow housing and landlord-tenant laws (ignorance is no excuse). Federal law covers lead paint and asbestos. Nationwide rules are set by the Civil Rights Act, Fair Housing Act, Americans With Disabilities Act, Fair Credit Reporting Act. State law typically regulates rent increase notices, security deposits, right of entry for landlord, housing standards, rental rules, repairs and maintenance, and evictions. Local ordinances cover much the same legal landscape, but tend to put a finer point to building codes, health and safety issues, eviction, etc.

Here are some issues that may — or may not — be ruled by your local laws. Also, your business can be impacted by court decisions ("case law") that interpret local, state and federal laws:

- ▶ Does local law provide for additional "protected groups" for fair housing beyond federal law, such as elderliness (55+), occupation, income source, immigration status, etc.?
- ▶ Are landlords forced to remodel for disabled access — or allow the tenant to remodel?
- ▶ Can the landlord keep all or some application fee or must he or she return the entire fee to a rejected applicant?
- ▶ Is the landlord allowed to collect the last month's rent in advance?
- ▶ Must the landlord give dated receipts for each rent payment?
- ▶ When can the landlord keep or must return security/damage deposits?
- ▶ Do local rules require the landlord to put deposits in an interest-bearing escrow account and pay the tenant accrued interest at the end of the lease?
- ▶ Must the landlord offer first right of refusal to a renter if the building is to be sold?
- ▶ Are there Fair Housing Act exemptions for landlords who rent only one, two or three rooms/units in their own homes?
- ▶ Do local rent-control rules apply to your building?
- ▶ Does your area require window guards, door peep scopes, recycling, removal of lead paint?
- ▶ Are local landlords required to supply screens, storm windows, blinds or window coverings?

◆ ◆ ◆

Essential Takeaway

Essential Takeaway: Get a good, local landlord-tenant lawyer on your team early. Not only will you want to comply with all local, state and federal laws from the get go, you'll also want the lawyer to review your lease, and maybe your advertising, tenant screening and record keeping. Be sure to have a written agreement of lawyer's fees and expectations. To find a legal specialist ask your mentor, investor network, landlord association or local housing authority.

◆ ◆ ◆

What Landlords Must Know About Anti-Discrimination Rules

To be a smart landlord, you must understand the federal, state and local laws against illegal discrimination when advertising for, interviewing and selecting renters.

When it comes to advertising, (including written, oral statements and pictures), federal Fair Housing rules forbid indicating a preference, limitation or discrimination based on race, color, sex, national origin, familial status (married, single, divorced or number of children), disabilities or religion. What's more, you can't use publications or other media that are accessible only to limited groups.

Follow these guidelines in pursuing good tenants for your rental:

Describe the property, not the people. Focus on the property and its features, not the background of tenants. Avoid some of these doozies that have been ruled discriminatory:

- ▶ "Desirable for Spanish-speaking individual"
- ▶ "Perfect for working females"
- ▶ "Walking distance to mosque"
- ▶ "Handicapped welcome"
- ▶ "Membership approval required"
- ▶ "Fraternity men need not apply"
- ▶ "Adult building, no children"
- ▶ "No Social Security Insurance; employed only"
- ▶ "No drinkers, smokers, migrant workers"
- ▶ "Not suitable for disabled, physically fit only"
- ▶ "Adult living, adults only, empty nesters, golden agers, mature couple, mature individual, older person, senior discount" discriminate unless the housing is specifically designed for elderly or 80% of units are occupied by 55 or older tenants.
- ▶ "Female roommate," "male housemate" terms discriminate unless relating to shared living quarters, not an individual unit.

Smart Tips To Choose Tenants Wisely

🖢 **Advertise.** The Internet has spawned numerous classifieds websites for renters from Craigslist, Backpage, Oodle, Rent.com, Apartments.com, RentoMeter.com and many others. *Smart Tip:* Become a student of syndication sites that renters frequent such as ListHub, Postlets and vFlyer to keep a finger on your local market pulse. In many markets, local newspapers and apartment magazines reach renters effectively.

● **Recruit.** Ask friends, family members and neighbors if they know of anyone looking for a rental. Be careful, though; renting to friends or relatives can make life difficult if disagreements arise later. One of the safest ways to find good tenants is through a reputable renters' service, which can advertise your property, screen applicants and refer people to you for a fee.

● **Applications and screening.** Make sure your application asks for all the information you need. Ask applicants for legal identification and income, then verify the information. One guideline for income is a gross income at least 3.5 times higher than annual rent. Ask for satisfactory personal and former-landlord recommendations. Ask questions about issues that are important to you using a uniform checklist, such as pets, parking (number and type of vehicles), smoking areas, motorcycles, waterbeds, large appliances, noise, outdoor cooking equipment, alterations, running a business from the unit, car repairs, extra storage space, occupancy limits, subletting procedure, etc., as long as they are within the law. Be sure your lawyer vets this checklist before your first use to avoid potential discrimination issues.

● **Be tough.** Check out renters thoroughly before signing a lease. You can reject a tenant for legitimate reasons, such as a history of bad debt/poor credit, former eviction, poor references, certain criminal convictions and not being able to afford the rent or false information on application, as long as you treat all applicants the same.

● **Credit reports.** You can ask applicants to submit their credit reports with their application or order a copy of the applicant's report directly from a credit reporting agency, with permission. (To order a credit report directly from one of the three major credit reporting agencies, contact *http://www.TransUnion.com*; *http://www.Equifax.com*; or *http://www.Experian.com*.) It is illegal to order a credit report on another person without that person's written permission. Many rental-application forms include language authorizing the landlord to obtain a credit report about the applicant.

❖ ❖ ❖

Essential Takeaway: *Exhibit fairness with a first-come, first-served selection — after checking references and credit. Use the same application form, same checklist, ask everyone for an application deposit, and treat all applicants the same.*

Essential Takeaway

❖ ❖ ❖

Develop An Iron-Clad Lease That Meets Your Needs And Property Specifics

Leases are as unique as every property and every investor. Beyond the "boiler plate" basics, be sure to have your lease reviewed by an experienced local attorney who specializes in real estate law. Not only does a lease or agreement specify the terms and conditions but it also gives you a legal basis to enforce rental policies — which may ultimately mean eviction.

Common issues:

- ▶ **Advance rent:** Collect last month rent against tenant leaving without notice, or use security deposit.
- ▶ **House rules:** Smoking, keys, property care, appliance use, noise, overnight visitors becoming co-tenants, maximum occupants, etc.
- ▶ **Lease change:** Process to make mutually agreeable changes to lease in writing.
- ▶ **Lease period:** One year? Longer? Renewal procedure?
- ▶ **Maintenance:** Any tasks required of tenant.
- ▶ **Parking:** Restrictions on vehicles. Number, type, parking location (such as not on lawn).
- ▶ **Payment:** Will you accept check, money order, cash, online or PayPal-like account?
- ▶ **Penalties:** Late-payment-fee definition. How much? Bounced check penalty. Attorney's fees paid by tenant.
- ▶ **Pets:** Allowed? If so, weight limit or acceptable breeds? Pet deposit.
- ▶ **Repairs:** Should renters pay first $25 or $50?

▶ **Security deposit:** How much? Rules for applying deposit to repairs and refund?

▶ **Sub-letting:** Permitted? If so, notification or lease change?

▶ **Termination:** Period of time required for notice to terminate. Termination triggers.

▶ **Utilities:** Landlord or tenant name on accounts. Who pays water/gas/sewer separate from electricity, telephone, cable TV?

▶ **Vacate notice:** Date required and penalty if "late" notice.

Normal Wear And Tear Versus Security-Deposit Damages

Landlords can use security deposits to repair damage but not normal wear and tear. So, what's the difference? Damage comes from accidents, unreasonable use, carelessness, theft or intentional alterations. Wear and tear comes from ordinary comings and goings. Typically, landlords may charge tenants for cleaning or repairs needed to restore the unit to the same condition as at the time of move-in. *Smart Tip:* Do a "move in" inspection with the tenant and use an "inspection checklist" to note problems. Take photos. Both sign and date the checklist. Keep the original and give your tenant a copy. At the end of the lease, use the same checklist during a "move out" inspection, and discuss any damage.

Use the "move in" walk-through as a tenant orientation. Identify common areas. Demonstrate appliances, heating and AC, security systems, smoke alarms, fire extinguishers, circuit breaker, main cut-offs for water, gas, electricity, operate fireplace flue and talk about trash collection and recycling, cable/Internet services, mail delivery and local emergency services and amenities. Strongly encourage timely repair requests (don't let a leak go for months).

◆ ◆ ◆

Essential Takeaway

Essential Takeaway: When things go badly, remember there are options. If the problem is illegal activity (drug dealing, gambling, prostitution), call the police. Police can arrest tenants but they do not have the right to evict them. Consider mediation (neutral third party helps find mutual resolution) or arbitration (neutral party hears case and makes a determination which, if agreed upon, is binding). Both are inexpensive alternatives to going to court. Another out-of-court solution is to release a tenant from the lease if he or she leaves voluntarily, perhaps with you offering to waive unpaid rent/late penalties for quick departure.

◆ ◆ ◆

SMART STRATEGIES TO RUN THE BUSINESS OF BEING A LANDLORD

Managing your real estate rental business as well as you manage the value of your properties will be essential.

How To Pick The Just-Right Rent Amount

The perfect rent amount does three things: (1) covers your operating expenses, (2) is competitive with comparable properties in the area and (3) provides a reasonable return on your investment.

● **Cost Approach:** Total all your projected costs and pick a rent that pays them. Expenses include:

- ▶ **Mortgage** (principal, interest and private mortgage insurance (PMI) if your down payment is less than 20%)

- ▶ **Property taxes, insurance** (at least, hazard insurance for damages from fires, storms or motor vehicles; and liability protection if anyone is hurt on the premises. Consider also: tenant relocation coverage if the property is uninhabitable; flood insurance; coverage for rent loss from fire or disasters; bonding if collected rents are stolen; mortgage credit life insurance to pay off the loan if you die)

- ▶ **Maintenance services** (trash, snow, yard, condo or homeowner association fees, carpet cleaning, rental equipment; estimating 2% of total property value for annual maintenance is one formula)

- ▶ **Repairs and replacements** (from gutters, windows, doors, drywall, light bulbs, tools and supplies to major appliances)

- ▶ **Utilities** (if tenant doesn't pay; water, gas, sewer, electric, Internet, cable)

- ▶ **Admin costs** (advertising, property management, accounting and tax prep, legal, business license tax, permits, travel, office supplies, unreimbursed casualty losses from theft, damage)
- ▶ **Planned rehab or improvements** (outdoor painting, driveway repaving, wiring, plumbing, additions, etc.)
- ▶ **Vacancy reserve** (5% is common but lost rent of 1 month = 12%, 2 months = 16%, 3 months = 25%; expect a short-term vacancy to clean up between tenants, and half-month rent expense if tenant uses a real estate agent to find a rental and another half month if a real estate agent screens tenants)
- ▶ **Return on investment** (5% to 8% is considered good)
- ▶ **Emergency reserve** (perhaps 3 months expenses for the unexpected, from being sued or an eviction to unexpected major repairs)

◆ ◆ ◆

Essential Takeaway

Essential Takeaway: Expenses are in your control more than market rents. If a rent that covers expenses is too high, then reduce expenses by making a higher down payment, using different financing, buying lower-maintenance property, spreading reserves over multiple properties, or staging the maintenance (if complete exterior painting costs are too much, paint the trim, doors, shutters and leave the rest for another time).

◆ ◆ ◆

💬 **Market Approach:** Rents out-of-line in an area can mean you have difficulty attracting tenants. The key is to compare like properties (single-family, townhouse, condo/apartment) because rents will vary. Use a common denominator to compare apples to apples, such as bedrooms/baths, total rooms or square feet. Build your own radius analysis by mapping data you collect using rents published online or in classifieds. Ask prospective tenants for addresses and rents they have looked at in the area and what media they used. Larger buildings and communities may charge a premium for amenities. Look for a middle to upper-middle sweet spot of optimum rent. *Smart Tip:* Be aware that some landlords price low, perhaps by foregoing amenities, to beat out competitors. Other landlords price high to attract renters willing to pay for luxury. Yet another strategy is to offer rent "specials" that feature a rent that looks like a deal, such as $975 instead of $1,000.

Dumb Rent-Setting Mistakes To Avoid

📢 **Do** revisit your pricing annually to reflect the market and local economic conditions, plus re-analysis gives you a reason to explain to tenants why you are increasing rent.

📢 **Do** base your rent on a thorough study of local comparables, not on guesstimates, formulas or hearsay.

📢 **Do** raise rents at appropriate time, typically at lease expiration, and give proper written notice to tenants as required by state or local law (may vary 10 to 60 days). Month-to-month agreements can generally raise rent as often as you want with proper notice.

📢 **Do** follow the rules if your jurisdiction has rent control that puts limits on how much and how often you can raise the rent.

📢 **Do** be aware if your area allows mid-lease "escalator clauses" that permit you to raise rent or collect surcharge for increases in property taxes or utilities.

Keep Your Paperwork

To properly account for your investment and to settle any disputes that could occur with tenants, retain:

▶ Copies of ads placed to attract applicants.

▶ Tenant files: leases, tenant applications, credit and employment reports on tenants, signed move-in and move-out inspection checklists, correspondence, complaints made by or about the tenant.

▶ Detailed records and receipts of all expenses associated with the property and tenant.

▶ Repair requests and repairs made.

▶ Organized records kept in deduction categories that the IRS allows to ease return preparation at tax time.

▶ Canceled checks and statements from a separate business checking account or credit card to pay for expenses separately and to keep records straight.

Costly Landlord Mistakes To Avoid

Mistake #1: Living with bad tenants and no-income vacancies.

Solution: Not to be glib, but the best way to avoid bad tenants is not to rent to them in the first place. Do a thorough credit check, employment check and present and previous landlord check on applicants before you accept them. Meet them in person to tour the place. Get information for a fallback plan if their rent is not forthcoming, such as parents, employer, military commander. A strong lease is essential.

Mistake #2: Hoping not to get caught cutting corners on landlord laws.

Solution: Don't risk it. Imagine a problem tenant who you want to evict. What is the tenant's lawyer's countersuit? That the tenant ("victim") rightfully withheld rent payments because required repairs were not made and is suing for damages because the landlord's negligence or retaliation violated this or that housing ordinance? Avoid this mistake and costly litigation.

Property Management May Be The Answer To Late-Night Headaches

Select the level of property management you want. DIY investors can contract for "lease only" services with a property manager. Lease-only includes advertising the property for rent, screening prospective renters, checking applications and getting a signed lease. Tenant-acquisition prices vary, of course, but a common fee is a half-month's to one-month's rent (half a month is 4% of annual rent). The cost of advertising and credit reports may be additional. You can either hire a part-time employee or contract with a property-management company. In some areas, being a property manager requires a real estate or other license.

On the other hand, property management services — that typically cost between 3% to 15% of collected rents — can range from cafeteria-style selected tasks to full-service. At the full-service end, commonly the cost is 8% of rental income when the investor pays the mortgage or 10% or more when the property manager is responsible for paying the mortgage.

Know The Services A Top Property Manager Can Provide

The range of specific responsibilities a Certified Property Manager (CPM) is assigned are clearly individual to each investor and property. Services in a property-manager agreement can include:

▶ Determine the optimal rental price after property inspection and research of comparable area rentals.

▶ Advise on practical property improvements that could bring a higher rent.

▶ Advertise for tenants, qualifying and screening the right ones, and get lease signed.

▶ Resolve day-to-day problems and maintain tenant relations.

▶ Provide inspection reports when the tenant moves in, is about to move out and after move-out.

▶ Hold security deposits and the escrow interest account, and handle disbursements as required by law.

▶ Collect rent, approve bills, deduct expenses, and disburse funds to investor.

▶ Take late-night calls for maintenance issues and arrange for service as needed.

▶ Keep records of tenant complaints and repair requests, including dated outcomes.

▶ Maintain and repair property at minimal cost practical to uphold property value and standards. Get approval for repairs over agreed limit, such as $150, and forward invoice to investor for payment and records.

▶ Supply regular operating statements, perhaps monthly, quarterly or annually.

▶ Communicate with the investor on all necessary topics, including possible need for eviction of problem tenant.

You'll specifically want to:

🗩 Interview individual(s) responsible for your property, such as an account manager or handyman.

🗩 Review proof of on-site individual's past experience, credentials, driving record, credit history, criminal background (if any).

● Check company's insurance, business licenses, bonds against employee theft.

● Consider an insurance bond for theft coverage by thief or property manager.

● Detail manager's responsibilities, compensation and termination clause in contract.

Once you have purchased the property, found reliable tenants and managed the property for cash flow and value, the day will come when you'll want to cash out. You'll find more on exactly how to do that smartly in the next — and last — Chapter 7: CASH OUT.

Chapter 6 Roundup

Smart Essentials MANAGEMENT ::
What You Have Learned

▶▶ How to be a successful landlord.
▶▶ Get on the right side of the law.
▶▶ What landlords must know about anti-discrimination rules.
▶▶ Smart tips to choose tenants wisely.
▶▶ Develop an iron-clad lease that meets your needs and property specifics.
▶▶ Normal wear-and-tear versus security-deposit damages.
▶▶ Smart strategies to run the business of being a landlord.
▶▶ How to pick the just-right rent amount.
▶▶ Dumb rent-setting mistakes to avoid.
▶▶ Costly landlord mistakes to avoid.
▶▶ Property management may be the answer to late-night headaches.
▶▶ Know the services a top property manager can provide.

CHAPTER 7

CASH OUT

In this chapter, you will learn smart ways to:

1. Time the right moment to cash out your investment.

2. Use equity buildup to trigger your profit-taking strategies.

3. Select from five ways to cash out that fit your investment goals.

SMART STRATEGIES TO MAXIMIZE YOUR PROPERTY'S VALUE

When it comes time to cash out and sell your property, potential investor buyers will want to know (1) number of units, (2) rental amounts, (3) occupancy rates (90% occupancy is 10% vacancy), and (4) maintenance costs. How much an investment buyer will pay is based on those factors, plus area sales prices of comparable properties.

Smart buyers examine maintenance expenses with a laser beam. Very low or non-existent expenses may be a red flag for big repairs to come. Very high costs may be a red flag for structural or system defects (the exception is recent major repairs or improvements such as roof, furnace, AC, new fence, driveway repaving and energy-saving improvements for efficient appliances, doors, windows, water heater, etc.) *Smart Tip:* Put the real estate first. If a property is well-maintained, it gives renters a reason to stay—and your investment buyer a reason to pay top dollar.

Another green flag for buyers is regular inspections, an energy audit and preventive maintenance that extends appliance life or takes care of small repairs before they become big projects.

SMART WAYS TO TAKE CASH OUT OF YOUR PROPERTY

It bears repeating that value in real estate is generated in a number of ways.

- ▶ You get cash from monthly rents.
- ▶ You get tax savings from depreciation and other deductions, which you can put in your pocket year round by adjusting your tax withholding.

▶ You'll have long-term appreciation going for you when you buy smart.

▶ You'll see equity build up from loan pay down.

▶ Plus, when you invest cash flow — or pay down an equity loan — you'll see growth in your other investments and your cash too.

There will come a time when you've built up enough equity in a property that you decide you want to put that equity to work. Knowing when to cash out an investment is essential. Do it right and you'll have cash in hand for other investments or expenses or to use as a down payment on other rental properties. Remember the *Essential Takeaway* from Chapter 1: BLUEPRINT: Owning more less-expensive properties is better than owning a few more-costly ones.

| Timing Your Moment To Cash Out |

One trick to riding the highs and lows of real estate markets is to keep an eye on local supply and demand indicators. Watch existing home sales, plus new-home building permits, mortgage defaults, foreclosures and interest rates so you can buy on the low end of a price cycle and sell near the top. Here are the four phases of every real estate cycle:

1. **Development:** Builders build to meet a demand. This is a good time to sell.

2. **Over-building:** The economy slows down. Demand drops, but builders complete construction underway.

3. **Adjustment:** Developers and lenders curtail new construction starts.

4. **Acquisition:** The economy picks up. Buyers start shopping again. This is a good time to buy, while prices are down and sellers are anxious to sell.

Watch local unemployment rates. Joblessness trending down means the resale market will be trending up. Watch the local housing market. Lower inventories and rising prices that reflect a seller's market mean it's a smart time to sell. Watch the rental market. When vacancy rates are falling and rents are rising, other investors will pay top dollar for your property.

Most important: Take your own pulse as an investor. Times change. Portfolios change. Income needs change. The essential time to cash in your investment is when you are ready — regardless of the market. One smart technique to know when the time is right is an "equity target" strategy.

USE EQUITY BUILDUP TO TRIGGER PROFIT TAKING

At last, equity buildup — the difference between the property value and the outstanding loan balance — triggers the right time to profit from your investment real estate. For example: When a $100,000 property that was purchased with $10,000 down and financed by a $90,000 loan reaches $120,000 in value, equity is $30,000 ($120,000 less $90,000 = $30,000). (To keep things simple, we have not included the equity increase from monthly principal payoffs that also increase your equity.)

Some smart investors set an "equity target," when write-offs from depreciation have run out — or the ratio of principal-to-interest payments no longer provides large mortgage interest deductions. Both stages dramatically reduce your leverage. In our example, the $100,000 property bought with $10,000 down means a loan to value of 90% ($90,000 divided by $100,000 = 90% LTV). Equity increases as the property appreciates until loan-to-value, in our example, becomes 75% ($90,000 divided by $120,000 = 75% LTV). Put in leverage lingo, your equity (leverage) has increased from 10% to 25%. Bingo. You've hit your 25% equity target, and it's time to take profits from equity. (As before, with principal paydown you may reach a higher equity target even faster than in this example.)

◆ ◆ ◆

Essential Takeaway

Essential Takeaway: *Appreciation can go on forever, literally. That's why some investors advise against ever selling a property. Why? Even after removing cash with an equity loan or cash-out refinance, your investment continues to grow more valuable as its potential sale price goes up. Smart investors know you can continue to realize appreciation gains even while transferring cash into new investments. Work with your investment real estate agent or accountant for advice on any cut-off points for depreciation or interest deductions that make it more sensible to sell the property than hold it.*

◆ ◆ ◆

5 Smart Strategies To Take Your Money And Run

📍 Strategy #1: Equity loan or HELOC payoff.

One option is to borrow against the equity in the property by using an equity loan or home-equity line of credit (HELOC). This cash can become the foundation for an expansion of your real estate investments. *Smart Tip:* Investors who used an outside equity loan for their investment down payment, use positive cash flow to pay down that original equity loan gradually until the day the renewed credit gives them available cash to invest in another property using the original credit line or loan. Although this strategy does not take out an equity loan on the investment property per se, the cash outcome is the same. This payoff strategy works especially well when cash flow is healthy.

📍 Strategy #2: Cash-out refinance.

With the refinance strategy, you keep the property but simply increase your leverage with a new tax-free loan. Talk with your trusted lender to determine whether it is best to refinance the entire first trust or obtain a commercial second-trust mortgage for a portion of the equity (Strategy #1). Either way, the new loan puts cash in your pocket tax-free (until sale later). You can use the cash for other purposes, improve the property to maintain value or increase rental income. Or, as many investors do, you can reinvest the cash into a down payment on another property that suits your goals. That last move requires no additional outlay beyond the proceeds realized from refinancing. Sweet.

- ▶ New market value: $120,000
- ▶ Old loan balance: $90,000
- ▶ Equity available for refinancing: $30,000 (less LTV requirements of lender)

📍 Strategy #3: Defer taxes with a 1031 exchange.

Rather than pay taxes on profits from the sale of an income-producing property, you can defer taxation by exchanging a qualified property for another "like-kind" property. It's called a 1031 exchange (also, "tax-deferred exchange"), named after Internal Revenue Code (IRC) section 1031.

Here are the essentials involved in a tax-deferred property exchange. *Smart Tip:* Because of the complexities and possible tax consequences of this type of transaction, be sure to consult a tax professional and/or a real estate attorney *before* attempting to execute a 1031 exchange.

What types of property can be exchanged? Real estate qualified for a tax-deferred exchange includes improved or unimproved property held for income, investment or business purposes. Both the old ("relinquished") property and the new ("replacement") property would have to fall within that definition for the transaction to be a qualified "like-kind" exchange.

You could, for example, exchange unimproved land for an improved property you intend to use as an investment or for your business — but not as your residence. Or, you could exchange ownership of one qualified property for ownership of multiple like-kind properties — and vice versa. A number of possibilities are available — as are a variety of limitations.

Can I take some money out of the transaction by investing in a property of lower value? To have a valid tax-deferred exchange, you must exchange the old property for a property of equal or greater value. If at the conclusion of the transaction you receive any cash, cash equivalents or non-like-kind property, you will owe capital gains taxes.

Also note, a 1031 exchange only defers taxation until such time as you sell the replacement property and take the money.

Can I simply sell one property and buy another? No. To reap the tax break, there must be an exchange, not just a sale and purchase of otherwise qualified properties. The law requires that the exchange must be properly executed through an exchange agreement serviced by a "qualified intermediary" according to a specific process and timetable defined by the tax code.

What is a qualified intermediary? Sometimes called a "facilitator" or "accommodator," a qualified intermediary (QI) functions as a middleman between you (the exchangor) and the buyers and sellers of the properties involved. Because you are not allowed to take physical possession or "constructive receipt" of the proceeds of the sale of your old property, the QI holds all the cash from the exchange until it is transferred to the seller of the replacement property. The QI facilitates the acquisition and transfer of the properties, providing documentation to ensure the exchange meets tax-code requirements. Your "exchange agreement" with the QI limits access to proceeds during the exchange, and may stipulate other services provided for an agreed-upon fee.

A QI must be an independent third party to the exchange. Neither you, your buyer nor the seller can serve as a QI in your exchange, nor can anyone who in the previous two years has been your employee, attorney, accountant, investment broker, real estate agent/broker or relative.

Be aware, there are no licensing requirements for QIs and the industry is largely unregulated. Because the QI is entrusted to hold all the funds involved in your 1031 exchange, it is important you select one that is reputable, experienced, financially sound and bonded.

Is there more than one way to structure a 1031 exchange?
There are two basic types of real property exchanges, each conducted according to timetables and rules outlined by Internal Revenue Code (IRC) and Treasury regulations, and two additional types of temporary "parking" arrangements.

1. **Simultaneous Exchange:** This occurs when both your old property and your new property go to closing (or settlement) on the same day.

2. **Delayed Exchange:** Settlement is non-simultaneous, with closing on the old property occurring on a different day and before closing on the replacement property. With delayed exchanges, strict timing requirements must be adhered to. You must close on or formally identify a replacement property within 45 calendar days of closing on the old property. In addition, you must close on the identified replacement property by one of two deadlines, whichever is earlier:

   1. Within 180 calendar days of the transfer of the old property; or,

   2. By the due date of the income tax return for the tax year during which the old property was closed.

A number of other requirements apply to the delayed-exchange process. Be sure to discuss them with your tax and legal advisors.

Parking Arrangements — There are two types of parking arrangements:

1. **Reverse Exchange:** Your replacement property is closed before you find a buyer for your relinquished property.

2. **Improvement Exchange:** You make improvements to a new or existing replacement property, investing the exchange proceeds.

Under the "safe harbor" rules, you must complete these non-simultaneous exchanges within 180 calendar days of title transfer to an "exchange accommodation titleholder" (generally a separate entity, such as an LLC owned by the QI), and you must identify the property to be relinquished within 45 calendar days. Again, consult your qualified tax and legal advisors for all the details relating to reverse and improvement exchanges.

Mistake: Expecting to use your real estate agent to conduct a 1031 exchange. A real estate professional who has served you professionally within the two years prior to the exchange agreement is disqualified from serving as the QI in your 1031 exchange. Where your agent can be invaluable is in helping you identify buyers for the property you want to sell and in helping you locate qualified like-kind replacement property.

Solution: Especially if you are considering a delayed or reverse exchange, you'll want to have an experienced, well-networked real estate professional on your side helping you meet the 45-day identification and 180-day exchange-period deadlines. Knowing how 1031 exchanges work, your agent must be dedicated to ensuring the sale and purchase of your investment properties come off smoothly — and remain tax-deferred!

Essential FAQs About 1031 Exchanges

Do I use a real estate professional in a 1031 exchange? Yes. Most owners use an agent to list the old property for sale and to find a replacement property to buy.

Are my buyer (old property) and seller (replacement property) involved as part of the exchange? No. Only you and your QI are directly involved in the exchange. To your buyer and seller, their transactions are handled traditionally.

Is it best to line up both ends of the exchange (a buyer for my old property and a replacement property to buy) before I begin? Yes. It's good practice to be ready to complete both sides of your exchange to meet the 1031 time limits, but it's not required. Once the clock is ticking, however, it can be nerve wracking if both transactions are not lined up in advance to make the exchange go smoothly.

● Strategy #4: Sell property.

Understand that rental markets don't always cooperate. Perhaps lenders won't refinance at an acceptably high loan-to-value ratio, or the appraisal of market value is so low that refinancing is not a reasonable alternative, or you need the cash for an unexpected reason. Selling the property is the answer to take out maximum equity profits. Before you decide, you'll want to factor in selling expenses from brokerage fees, fix-up expenses, seller-paid discount points and perhaps vacancy in the transition.

Ask your investment real estate agent and accountant if selling expenses in your situation fit within the general rule of 9% – 11% of sales price. Also, remember that profits from sale will be taxed at capital-gains rates if the property was held for more than a year. Plus, you want to be sure to factor in adjustments for recapture of excess depreciation, which will add income (profit) to your taxable personal income (see the following example).

Crunch your numbers to estimate net proceeds from sale.

Smart investors take their calculations a step further by figuring the net proceeds of sale after tax. Basically, you subtract the costs of sale, mortgage balance, and any tax liability from the sale price to come up with a "net walk-away cash" figure. The calculations look like this:

▶ Sale Price: $120,000

Less:

▶ Costs of Sale: $12,000

▶ Mortgage Balance: $90,000

Proceeds Sub-total: $18,000

Less:

▶ Tax Liability[††]: $8,166

Net proceeds of sale after tax: $9,833 ($18,000 – $8,166 = $9,833)

> **[††] *Tax Liability***
> Tax liability is calculated in our example to be based on $29,166 taxable income x 28% marginal tax bracket = $8,166. The $29,166 taxable income figure ("recapture") comes from subtracting the allowed straight-line depreciation from the years of actual accelerated depreciation claimed ($68,055 accelerated less $38,889 straight-line = $29,166 taxable income). Again, these hypothetical figures are for illustration only.

🗨 Strategy #5: Installment Sale To Defer Taxes

Instead of taking the proceeds as a lump sum, some investors take back their equity in the form of a second or third mortgage to the purchaser. In today's market with more renters who lost their homes to foreclosure, getting financing from their landlord (also, "rent-to-buy," "lease-purchase"), rather than a lender, can be very attractive to some tenants. Essentially, you receive the equity over a period of time as installment payments plus interest, rather than one big check at settlement. You can structure the deal many ways.

One example: A written contract gives the tenant an option to buy the property at an agreed-upon price after an agreed-upon number of years. There may be an option-to-buy fee that can range from several hundred dollars to several thousand (say, 5% of home's value). An extra amount may be added to rent payments that can be applied to the future down payment or purchase price.

Why do this? The largest plus, besides receiving current income just like you enjoyed from rent, is benefiting from deferring your profits — and thus deferring capital-gains taxes. Remember, tax rules require that you must declare in the year of sale all depreciation for recapture. If you have an installment sale, you only have to report each installment payment that is a percentage of remaining profit from the entire sale. Essentially you pay capital gains on the installment payments, not the entire sale price. Sound complicated? Not really, but it takes some planning. Be sure to consult your tax advisor to weigh the implications.

CONGRATULATIONS!

In many areas of the country, American real estate is experiencing a convergence of unprecedented rental demand and affordable inventory, low interest rates and rising rents.

It bears repeating: The housing crash turned millions of foreclosed homeowners into renters. Millions more are underwater, delinquent or in default. Waves of downsizing baby boomers (10,000 a day turn 65) are opting to rent. Boomerangers...3 million young adults who lived with their parents during the Great Recession...are now moving out to rent on their own. Every year hundreds of thousands of new immigrants are renting until they can buy into the American dream of homeownership.

Simply put, millions of new renters will drive rental housing demand for years to come.

There you have it.

Today is one of the best times in a generation to buy investment real estate, especially single-family homes.

The stunning fact is *get rich steadily* strategies are paying off handsomely in this market.

So, Smartie, maybe it's the perfect time to grow your own real estate investment portfolio. Keep in mind our cardinal rule: The only thing better than one great rental investment is several great rental properties. When you do invest in your next rental, you'll be even smarter.

If you know someone who is planning to invest soon, pay it forward by recommending SMART ESSENTIALS FOR REAL ESTATE INVESTING.

Again, high five, Smartie!

Chapter 7 Roundup

Smart Essentials CASH OUT :: What You Have Learned

▶▶ Smart strategies to increase your property's value.
▶▶ How to time the right moment to cash out your investment.
▶▶ Use equity buildup to trigger profit taking.
▶▶ *Strategy #1:* Equity loan or HELOC payoff.
▶▶ *Strategy #2:* Cash-out refinance.
▶▶ *Strategy #3:* Defer taxes with a 1031 exchange.
▶▶ *Strategy #4:* Sell property.
▶▶ *Strategy #5:* Installment sale to defer taxes.

About The Series

SMART ESSENTIALS was written for you.

We know because you tell us. Our readers are smart, busy, capable people stressed by the fact that they only get one chance to get it right buying or selling real estate. You tell us on our *http://www.SmartEssentials.com* website and in your emails. You appreciate smart, useful, distilled information that goes straight to the point.

Certainly, our readers *can* swim through the tides of endless online articles searching for useful information. Certainly, our readers *can* slog through full length how-to books trying to glean the chapter here or there that they really need hidden in the general filler. But you're too smart for that. You appreciate concise ideas that can make you tens of thousands in profit when you sell real estate and save you thousands at the settlement table when you buy — or avoid costly mistakes you didn't have to make.

You want the information now. You want it smartly presented. You want it current for today's market. Mostly you want your information concise, concentrated and applicable to your situation.

💬 Like the stressed-out bride who thanked us for advising that soon-to-be-newlyweds start looking for a home three months *after* the wedding.

💬 Like the Canadian investor who appreciated learning that California charges a transfer tax on non-resident sales, so he bought in Nevada.

💬 Like the thankful divorced Dad who bought two extra bedrooms for sleepovers on custody weekends.

💬 And like the thankful parents who saved thousands over seven years (two serial college kids) by investing in rentable student housing because at their state university most students had to rent off-campus housing.

We also know most of our readers typically buy multiple SMART ESSENTIALS. Not only because most sellers are buyers and most buyers become sellers, but mostly because you have smart friends. You talk. Naturally. After all, you just spent the last few months consumed by one of the largest life-shaping transactions of your life. Who wouldn't need to vent?

That's why we wrote every SMART ESSENTIALS for you.

Let us know what you think. More important, when you run across one of those incredible little nuggets of street-smart wisdom during your transaction, email us or share it as a Smarties' Story on our website. We love your stories. And the thousands of other Smarties facing the same situation will thank you, too. Giving is sharing. And sharing is the best way we know to enhance love.

Looking forward to hearing from you!

Dan Gooder Richard
Series Editor

Dan Gooder Richard can be contacted at:

SMART ESSENTIALS
c/o Inkspiration Media
2724 Dorr Avenue, Suite 103
Fairfax, VA 22031
(703) 698-7750
Investing@SmartEssentials.com
http://www.SmartEssentials.com

About The Team

A venture the size of SMART ESSENTIALS requires an outstanding team. Dan Gooder Richard is the editor of SMART ESSENTIALS and author of INVESTING. Dan's first book, *REAL ESTATE RAINMAKER®: Successful Strategies for Real Estate Marketing,* was published by John Wiley & Sons in 2000. Dan's second book, *REAL ESTATE RAINMAKER®: Guide to Online Marketing,* was published by John Wiley & Sons in 2004. He is also creator of the RAINMAKER LEAD SYSTEM® now in use by thousands of real estate professionals nationwide. He and his wife, Synnove Granholm, founded GOODER GROUP® in 1983 and continue to manage the Fairfax, Virginia-based publisher of marketing materials for real estate and mortgage professionals. Hats off to Deb Rhoney, our managing editor and principal writer. She puts the smart into the essentials. Thanks to M. Anthony Carr, author of *Real Estate Investing Made Simple* (AMACOM, 2005) for his insightful edits. Amy Hausman, our marketing diva and writer, keeps the buzz going with every new publication. Special thanks to our web master, Tammy Waitsman, and our social media guru, Jesse Hickman, for making the online side of SMART ESSENTIALS truly click. Jane Rooney, our controller at Inkspiration Media, keeps us on track and on forecast. Stephanie Simmons keeps the service to members stellar and makes the smallest detail her mission. A special thanks to David Wu of DW Design, whose branding and graphic design makes us all look good. To the entire team at SMART ESSENTIALS — thank you — we couldn't do it without you!

SMARTIES' CREED

💬 **I will express my voice** at *http://www.SmartEssentials.com* and become part of the world's smartest communities.

💬 **I will help others get smarter for less.** I simply share with two. And they tell two. If we pay it forward 33 times, we can reach every person in the world.

💬 **I will keep up to date** and with one click, one post, one random act of selflessness, I will be smarter, happier, richer.

💬 **I can imagine** where everyone reading my voice did something today to improve others. The world would be a smarter place . . . and it all would be thanks to my original, selfless act to help others.

SMART TALK

The fact that you are reading this sentence tells us a lot about you. Clearly, you have a hunger for wisdom to increase your real estate investing smarts. Having gotten this far, it's likely you've got insights, experiences and questions of your own to share. Now it's time to reach out to other Smarties by sharing your answers and questions at the Smart Talk knowledge center: http://www.SmartEssentials.com. *We'll all be smarter for it!*

Pay it forward at *http://www.SmartEssentials.com* today!

More Titles In The Best-Selling SMART ESSENTIALS Series

💬 SMART ESSENTIALS FOR SELLING YOUR HOME
How To Get The Highest Price In The Shortest Time

💬 SMART ESSENTIALS FOR BUYING A HOME
How To Get The Best Price And The Lowest Payment

💬 SMART ESSENTIALS FOR REAL ESTATE INVESTING
How To Build Wealth In Rental Property Today

💬 SMART ESSENTIALS FOR BUYING FORECLOSURES
Finding Hidden Bargains For Home Or Profit

💬 SMART ESSENTIALS FOR COLLEGE RENTALS
Parent and Investor Guide To Buying College-Town Real Estate

www.ingramcontent.com/pod-product-compliance
Lightning Source LLC
Chambersburg PA
CBHW071438210326
41597CB00020B/3845